JUVENILE CAREWORKER

Resource Guide

American Correctional Association

The Honorable Helen G. Corrothers, President
James A. Gondles, Jr., Executive Director
Patricia L. Poupore, Director of Communications and Publications
Elizabeth Watts, Publications Managing Editor
Marianna Nunan, Assistant Editor
Kristen M. Miller, Editorial Assistant

Photo Credits

The American Correctional Association would like to credit the following for providing photographs for this publication. All other photographs are from ACA files.

Warren H. Albrecht (page 97)
Capitol Communication Systems, Inc. (cover, 9, 12, 15, 16, 17, 21, 23, 24, 31, 32, 35, 42, 49, 55, 58, 61, 65, 75, 78, 82, 89, 92, 98, 101, 102, 109, 111)

Charles J. Kehoe (39, 72, 105)
Robert E. Morris (52, 77, 85)
Sun West Services, Inc. (91)

ISBN 0-929310-78-0

Printed in the United States of America by Kirby Lithographic Company, Arlington, Va.

Contents

Acknowledgments

The American Correctional Association wishes to thank all the authors who contributed to this book, many who contributed freely of their time and professional expertise.

We are also grateful to those individuals who acted as reviewers and advisors in the editing of this book. For this we acknowledge Lloyd Mixdorf, Geno Natalucci-Persichetti, James Davis, John Sheridan, and Barbara Dooley.

Foreword

This *Juvenile Careworker Resource Guide* brings together the expertise of professionals in juvenile corrections to provide an overview of the role of the careworker in today's juvenile corrections system.

Juvenile corrections continues to evolve and to present new challenges to those who work in the field. In today's complex society permeated with drug abuse, homelessness, and poverty, juvenile offenders are more hostile and aggressive than ever before. In attempting to contend with negative social forces, institutions are emphasizing programming designed to give juveniles a chance to succeed once released to the community.

Litigation has made its mark in juvenile corrections by bringing attention to the issue of juvenile rights, particularly constitutional rights. It continues to be difficult for facilities to provide services required by law because many facilities must operate on tight budgets and few resources.

Health care and special needs services are also in the forefront of juvenile corrections. The high rate of drug abuse among juveniles has led to concerns about treating addiction and its resulting medical complications. Drug abuse and sexual promiscuity have made HIV and AIDS major concerns in juvenile facilities.

The information in this guide provides a general overview of the careworker's role. The information is not intended to be all encompassing or specific to a particular juvenile correctional system. It is important to remember that each juvenile correctional system has its own specific regulations and policies and that each facility's physical design dictates its operational procedures. The procedures and policies described in this publication may conflict with established agency policies or local statutory requirements. In those instances, local regulations and law must govern the actions of the individual employee. Keeping this in mind, this guide will prove to be a valuable introductory resource. When used in connection with the training provided by an individual correctional facility or agency, it can be the basis for an excellent understanding of the fundamentals of carework in juvenile corrections.

We are grateful to the many prominent authors and reviewers who gave their expertise and time in the preparation of this book.

James A. Gondles, Jr.
Executive Director
American Correctional Association

1

History of Juvenile Corrections

By Kimberly Konitzer

The history of juvenile corrections has been a long and convoluted experience in trial and error. Methods for dealing with delinquent juveniles have ranged from religious judgment to paternalistic protection. Prior to the Middle Ages, juveniles were subject to the same practice of "an eye for an eye" adults were. The history of juveniles' involvement in the justice system can be divided into five eras of practice: the English and American Experience (pre-1825), the Reformatory Period (1825–1899), the Juvenile Court Era (1899–1960), the Gault Era (1960–1980), and the Present Era (1980-present).

English and American Experience (Pre-1825)

In the Middle Ages, people decided what was right and wrong and how transgressions should be dealt with by consulting the church. Canon Law ruled the land, and everyone was subject to its teachings. Punishment came to juveniles just as it did to adults.

Kimberly Konitzer is a researcher/writer on juvenile issues for the Training and Contracts Division of the American Correctional Association.

Delinquent juveniles and adult offenders were subject to many of the same forms of punishment, including death by hanging, drowning, or burning at the stake. Delinquent juveniles and their adult counterparts were jailed in the same facilities; there was no separation by age for the incarcerated. However, there were a few guidelines for leniency when it came to the punishment of juveniles. For example, many courts held that offenders under the age of fourteen could not be executed for their crimes.

The Early English experience produced an important philosophy that soon took root in juvenile corrections. *Parens patriae*, the idea that the state must act as parent for the children under its jurisdiction, became prevalent and remained a driving force into the American experience.

Colonial Americans relied on the Puritan church and the family as the backbone of their society. Often, the most a juvenile had to fear in terms of punishment came from his or her family. Only after familial justice failed did the community become involved. Once in the hands of the community, juveniles were subject to many of the same penalties as adults. Committing major crimes could result in expulsion from the community or execution. The English concept of *parens patriae* did not come into widespread popularity in the United States until the 1800s.

Reform schools marked the beginning of a formal municipal interest in housing delinquent juveniles.

Reformatory Period (1825–1899)

With the onset of the Industrial Revolution in the 1800s, the demand for cheap labor increased dramatically, and able-bodied juveniles were the main source. Although juveniles were valued as a major element in the work force, many of them lived under poor, dehumanizing conditions. Population centers were forming in the cities, and the family structure began to deteriorate. Juveniles were experiencing a level of independence they never knew before.

The state realized that it needed to respond to the fact that parents could no longer control their children as they once could. The onset of *parens patriae* saw the responsibility for the proper upbringing of juveniles fall to the legal system. Institutions were created by communities and concerned citizens' groups to deal with issues involved in the development of the nation's

juveniles. These institutions, which were called refuge houses, were meant to take in wayward juveniles and promote proper values normally taught by the juveniles' own families.

The first institution established for juvenile offenders in the United States, the New York City House of Refuge, opened in 1825. Although houses of refuge were established to protect the young from the perils of society, they soon degenerated and became warehouses for society's throwaways. Conditions in the houses of refuge often worsened the delinquency of their wards. Delinquent juveniles were seen as wicked, and the houses of refuge sought to change them or at least keep them off the streets. Toward the end of their popularity, the houses of refuge began to send delinquent juveniles as "apprentices" to farms or other rural areas that needed another body for manual labor. This practice became known as "placing out."

Placing out was meant to keep juveniles busy,

thus keeping them out of trouble and providing cheap labor for rural areas of the country at the same time. Soon business owners in large urban areas became upset with this practice. They felt that they were losing a valuable source of inexpensive labor for their factories. This sentiment, coupled with the discovery of grossly exaggerated claims of success from the houses of refuge and the placing out movement, led to the development of the reform school.

Municipal and state governments began to enter the reform school business to indoctrinate delinquent juveniles with values appropriate for successful living. These facilities concentrated on formal training to reform juveniles from their delinquency. Reform schools marked the beginning of a formal municipal interest in housing delinquent juveniles.

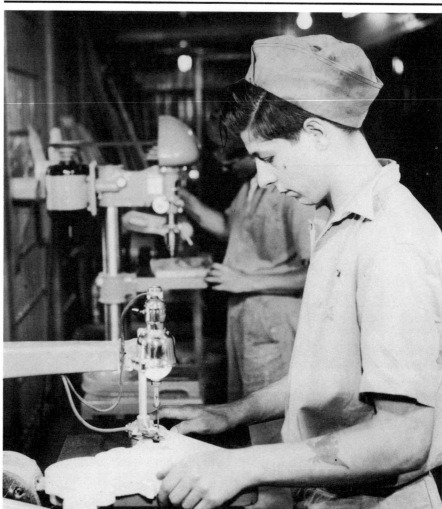

Facilities concentrated on formal training to reform juveniles from their delinquency during the reformatory period.

During the period of the Civil War, adult jails and penitentiaries were almost empty, while reform schools were bursting at the seams. After the war, many reform schools were in fierce competition with other government agencies for funds, and as a result, many had to operate on deficit budgets. This caused many reform schools to eliminate anything that was not absolutely necessary. Juvenile institutions began to resemble human warehouses just as before. Once again, a major change in the juvenile justice system became necessary.

Juvenile Court Era (1899–1960)

The Juvenile Court Act, which was passed by the Illinois legislature in 1899, officially established the first juvenile justice system in the United States. The act established a juvenile court division within the Illinois court system and gave it exclusive jurisdiction over juveniles who were delinquent, neglected, or dependent.

News of the success of the Illinois Juvenile Court spread rapidly, and in the same year the Juvenile Court Act was adopted in Illinois, a juvenile court was organized in Denver. The idea went international when England passed the Children's Act of 1908. By 1931, thirty nations had some form of juvenile court. By 1945, every state in America had laws for a juvenile court.

This new court classified all juvenile procedures as civil instead of criminal. The juvenile courts usually circumvented the formalities of the criminal process because, at the time, it was thought that this treatment gave juveniles more leeway by focusing on the juvenile instead of the offense. Unfortunately, juveniles ended up losing many of their rights instead of gaining new rights. This situation continued until the 1960s when *In Re Gault* appeared before the U.S. Supreme Court.

Gault Era (1960–1980)

The 1960s brought about a general concern for the civil rights of all people. There was a growing dissatisfaction with many of America's institutions—juvenile courts included. Reformers began to examine juvenile courts to see where they could be improved and to identify cases that would help them to do so.

In the course of ten years, the Supreme Court would hand down five major decisions affecting the course of juvenile justice in the United States. The most far-reaching, and perhaps the most well-known, was *In Re Gault* in 1967.

In Re Gault involved a fifteen-year-old-boy, Gerald Gault, who was charged with making obscene phone calls. The Arizona Juvenile Court committed Gault to a state training school until he was twenty-one years old. If Gault had been an adult, the maximum punishment would have been a fifty-dollar fine or two months in jail. His parents appealed the decision to the U.S. Supreme Court.

The U.S. Supreme Court overturned the decision of the Juvenile Court in Arizona. The Court held that as a juvenile, Gault was entitled to a lawyer, whether he could afford one or not. Juveniles and their parents also became entitled to written notice of charges. The Court held that juveniles are entitled to cross-examine their accusers and that they are protected against self-incrimination. In short, *In Re Gault* provided juveniles with some of the due process rights afforded adults.

The Gault case, in addition to other cases of the time, helped limit the discretion of the juvenile court. They established that juvenile cases would be heard in a court of law with all of the accompanying safeguards. In addition to the Supreme Court, legislators also did their part to reform the system.

The President's Commission Report in 1967 suggested a number of reforms that include the four Ds:

- *decriminalization* of juvenile courts
- *diversion* of offenders to community resources
- *due process* for juveniles as for adults
- *deinstitutionalization* of juvenile offenders

In 1973 the National Advisory Commission on Criminal Justice Standards and Goals also recommended the four Ds. Legislation carried out the four Ds in the form of the Juvenile Justice and Delinquency Prevention Act of 1974, which created the Office of Juvenile Justice and Delinquency

---

The Gault case, in addition to other cases of the time, helped limit the discretion of the juvenile court.

Prevention. The Act stipulated that all states had to (1) remove status offenders from locked detention facilities and (2) stop committing status offenders to training schools. If the states did not comply, they would forfeit federal funding for state juvenile delinquency programs.

The late 1960s and early 1970s witnessed a deinstitutionalization movement whereby hard-core delinquents were committed to training schools and others were diverted to the community. The enthusiasm for community-based corrections was so great that some began to feel that large-scale, secure training schools would soon become obsolete in juvenile justice. Today, the public is no longer quite as enthusiastic about community programs as it was in the late 1960s and early 1970s.

Present Era (1980–Present)

Juvenile corrections in today's world operates in an atmosphere of constant change. Accountability has increased as a programmatic concern, and this concern will probably continue. Some jurisdictions are increasing the number of transfers of juveniles to the adult criminal justice system in response to the public's demand for harsher punishment for juveniles who commit serious crimes. Community service also seems to be playing a larger role in the range of juvenile justice options. Opinions and policies will continue to change when it comes to juvenile delinquency and the juvenile justice system.

Specific practices are under as much scrutiny as broad-based philosophies in the juvenile justice system. The public has a strong desire for community protection, whether it be through incarceration or through intensive monitoring. The availability of funds is the bottom line for many communities. Concerns such as public safety, education, and delinquency all take a back seat to what the jurisdiction can afford.

In terms of correctional philosophy, modern corrections professionals are talking much more about education, skills training, and discipline as priorities than ever before. The words "rehabilitation" and "treatment" are heard less frequently when people talk about what is most important for juveniles in custody. Once again, this is also likely to change.

Another component in juvenile corrections that is constantly evolving is the juvenile offender. The issues and crises juveniles face in the modern world are changing the face of the average juvenile delinquent. Juveniles in the system today are more violent, more involved with illegal drugs and alcohol, younger, and more involved in gang activity than in the past. In addition to individual characteristics, a general shift in racial proportions of juveniles in the justice system has occurred. The number of minority juveniles being taken into custody and processed through the juvenile courts is rising much faster than the number of white juveniles for the same types of offenses.

One of the most noteworthy improvements in juvenile justice is the development of standards for juvenile justice facilities. The American Correctional Association's juvenile facility standards allow practitioners to gauge their activities against the level of professionalism necessary to ensure proper

---

Juveniles in the system today are more violent, more involved with illegal drugs and alcohol, younger, and more involved in gang activity than in the past.

---

treatment of juveniles in custody. ACA's accreditation process uses those standards as the basis by which it judges facilities in compliance and therefore worthy of accreditation. Accreditation is a source of pride in achievement for staff and administration alike. It shows them that they are doing their jobs well, while it gives them something to aim for in the future.

ACA's juvenile standards and accreditation process changes in the modern era have brought about a high level of professionalism among the ranks of juvenile justice practitioners. Along with these improvements has come a long list of new challenges facing juveniles in the system and the people who work with them.

2

Overview of the Juvenile Justice System

By William Taylor

The juvenile justice system is made up of several basic components that work together to carry out society's response to juvenile delinquent activity. This justice function is based on the right and responsibility of the state to act in the role of parent when the natural parents or guardians are unfit to perform their duties (*parens patriae*).

The basic components of the juvenile justice system can be identified as follows:

1. *Police deparments* are law enforcement agencies that come into most frequent contact with juvenile offenders. They have discretion about whether to handle cases informally or to take juveniles into custody and place them under the responsibility of the juvenile justice system.

2. *Detention facilities* are secure or nonsecure residential facilities used to hold juveniles pending release to a parent or guardian, pending a court hearing, awaiting disposition, or pending placement in a facility or program.

3. *Juvenile court* is the judicial body that assumes jurisdiction after a juvenile is taken into custody. The court determines whether a juvenile is delinquent and how the case should be resolved, e.g., turned over to the adult court, placed on probation, placed in juvenile corrections, or imposed sanctions other than confinement.

4. *Corrections* is the agency responsible for the confinement, rehabilitation, and/or reintegration of adjudicated juveniles. Corrections may also administer aftercare, which involves the community supervision of juveniles for a limited period of time after confinement.

5. *Community agencies* are dispositional alternatives for juveniles who may be placed in a nonsecure residential or day treatment program.

Complaint

The juvenile justice process begins with a complaint against a juvenile. A complaint is a written or an oral statement of the facts that allege a delinquent offense, noncriminal misbehavior, neglect, or abuse.

William Taylor is the American Correctional Association's project director for private-sector options for juvenile corrections.

Most jurisdictions prefer to have a written complaint because a complaint provides the basis for intake screening.

Taking a Juvenile into Custody

Many juveniles who come into contact with police are not referred to juvenile court. Of those actually taken into custody because of an alleged delinquent act, an average of 30 to 45 percent are either counseled and released or referred to community services. In some police departments, this diversion rate may exceed 70 percent.

Approximately 100,000 juveniles are held in custody on any given day. Many of these juveniles are held in juvenile detention facilities, which temporarily hold juveniles accused of committing a crime or an offense. The American Correctional Association, in its *Guidelines for the Development of Policies and Procedures: Juvenile Detention Facilities*, recommends that only the juveniles who fall under one of the following categories be detained in a secure facility:

- those who are fugitives from another jurisdiction

- those who request protection in writing and who may be in immediate danger of serious physical injury

- those accused of first- or second-degree murder

- those charged with a crime equivalent to a felony, such as manslaughter, rape, or aggravated assault

- those who are on probation

- those who have a record of willful failure to appear in court

- those who have a record of violent behavior that resulted in physical injury to others

- those who cannot be placed in a less restrictive facility to reduce the risk of flight or serious harm to property or to the physical safety of the juvenile or others

Status offenders (those accused of noncriminal misbehavior) and abused juveniles should not be placed in secure detention.

The police have the most frequent contact with juvenile offenders.

The police may take a juvenile who falls into one of these categories into custody and place the juvenile in detention or release the juvenile until the court date. In some jurisdictions, the facility's intake officer makes the decision to detain a juvenile. The decision, in either case, must be reviewed by a judge. According to ACA standards, any juvenile placed in detention must be seen by a judge within forty-eight hours. Laws on this turnaround time, however, differ from state to state. The judge decides whether the juvenile will be released or sent to a secure or less restrictive facility. If the juvenile is placed in a secure facility, ACA standards require that the judge review the case every ten days.

Intake

Once a complaint is received by an intake officer, the intake process begins. The type of intake process depends on the jurisdiction (i.e., state, county, or court system). Despite some operational differences between jurisdictions, the intake officer performs the same basic duties.

The detention intake officer examines the complaint to ensure the allegations are sufficient to bring the juvenile into court. For example, the officer determines whether the court has jurisdiction in the case. The examination ensures that a juvenile is not held on improper grounds or on erroneous allegations.

If the intake officer decides that the complaint is not sufficient, he or she may refer it back to the complainant for more information. If the intake officer has a legal question, the officer may consult an attorney from the prosecutor's office.

If the intake officer finds the complaint to be sufficient, the options are as follows:

- refer the juvenile to a social agency

- recommend to the prosecutor that a petition be filed

- implement other options specified in state laws

When an intake officer recommends that a petition be filed, the final determination on whether a complaint is legally sufficient and warrants further action usually rests with the prosecutor's office. In some jurisdictions, other agencies and/or individuals can file a complaint requiring a judicial hearing.

For delinquency cases, the intake officer should consider the following parameters:

- seriousness of the alleged offense

- role of the juvenile in the offense

- nature and number of contacts with the intake unit and juvenile court and the results of those contacts

- juvenile's age and maturity

- availability of appropriate services outside the juvenile justice system

For noncriminal misbehavior cases, the intake officer should consider the following parameters:

- seriousness of the alleged conduct and the circumstances in which it occurred

- age and maturity of the juvenile

- nature and number of contacts with the intake unit and juvenile court

- outcome of those contacts, including the outside services to which the juvenile and/or the family have been referred and the results of those referrals

- availability of appropriate services

- family situation in general

For neglect and abuse cases, the intake officer should consider the following parameters:

- seriousness of the alleged neglect or abuse and the circumstances in which it occurred

- age and maturity of the juvenile alleged to have been neglected or abused

- nature and number of contacts with the intake unit and the juvenile court the family has had

- outcome of those contacts, including the services to which the family has been referred and the results of those referrals

- availability of appropriate services outside the juvenile justice system that do not involve removal of the juvenile from the home

- willingness of the family to accept those services

- safety of the juvenile

Intake often acts as the gatekeeper of the juvenile justice system. Once an intake officer recommends a petition be filed, a juvenile enters the juvenile justice process.

Detention Facilities

A detention facility is a secure institution used for the temporary custody of juveniles accused or adjudicated of delinquent conduct who should not be placed in an open setting. Detention facilities are used to care for such juveniles following arrest, before adjudication, before disposition, and following disposition while awaiting transfer to the facility of placement. Detention facilities may also be used for the temporary custody of juveniles who are awaiting a hearing to change or enforce a dispositional order, extradition to a community with jurisdiction, or return to the residential facility from which they have escaped.

According to ACA standards, a juvenile should only be placed in a detention facility to protect the public, prevent self-injury, or ensure his or her presence at subsequent judicial hearings. The detention facility is usually the juvenile's first contact with the correctional system, and this initial

---

Once an intake officer recommends a petition be filed, a juvenile enters the juvenile justice process.

---

stay has a major affect on the juvenile. Detention facilities, therefore, should operate under policies and procedures based on professional standards.

Detention facilities provide many services for detained juveniles, including the following:

- security and control
- nutritious meals
- educational testing, if time allows
- medical and health care
- counseling—group and/or individual (as necessary)
- education
- communication—mail, visits, telephone calls
- recreational activities
- opportunities for religious contact or services
- citizen and volunteer participation
- release preparation and transfer programs

Secure detention facilities should remain the gateway to juvenile justice only for juveniles in serious trouble.

Juvenile Courts

Juvenile courts differ theoretically from criminal courts in many ways. Criminal courts determine the guilt or innocence of those accused of committing a crime. A guilty verdict results in a conviction. On the other hand, a juvenile found guilty in a juvenile court is usually adjudicated, meaning the court has found the juvenile to be delinquent.

The juvenile court has other distinguishing characteristics:

1. The court emphasizes treatment rather than punishment.

2. Court records are confidential.

3. The judge makes a disposition in a case instead of imposing a sentence.

4. The juvenile's needs, social background, and prior behavior are considered in making the disposition.

5. Juvenile cases are usually settled more quickly than adult cases. The unstructured nature of the juvenile court creates less litigation and thus speeds up the judicial process.

6. Juveniles sometimes receive shorter terms of confinement than adults for similar offenses.

Adjudicatory Hearing

The adjudicatory hearing is the process in which the juvenile court determines whether the juvenile is delinquent. The hearing is usually closed to the public to protect the juvenile's privacy.

A juvenile has the same right to due process as an adult in a criminal trial. In general, a juvenile has the right to the following:

- receive notice to be present at the adjudicatory hearing (and other proceedings)
- confront and cross-examine witnesses
- an impartial decision maker (the judge)
- counsel
- an open proceeding, if he or she so chooses

11

- appeal

- remain silent

The (state) prosecutor must prove beyond a reasonable doubt that the juvenile is guilty. If the prosecutor proves the juvenile's guilt, the court finds the juvenile delinquent.

Some juvenile court judges suspend the adjudicatory hearing and place the juvenile under supervision. Officers of the court monitor the juvenile. If the juvenile behaves well during the period of supervision, the judge dismisses the petition. If the juvenile gets into more trouble, however, the adjudicatory hearing is held. This process of supervision, called a continuance, gives the juvenile the opportunity to avoid adjudication as a delinquent and the resulting stigma attached to such a label.

At the dispositional hearing, the judge decides what disposition the juvenile will receive.

Dispositional Hearing

If a court finds a juvenile to be delinquent, a dispositional hearing is scheduled. At the hearing, the judge decides what disposition the juvenile will receive. This process is similar to sentencing in criminal court.

The judge determines the type of sanction to be imposed and the duration of the sanction in compliance with applicable laws. Nationally recognized criteria for the disposition decision recommend that the judge select the least restrictive disposition and time period consistent with the seriousness of the offense, the juvenile's role in the offense, the juvenile's age, and the juvenile's prior record.

The judge also selects the type of program—foster care, vocational training, drug treatment, etc.—the juvenile should be offered based on the juvenile's needs and interests. The correctional agency may select the specific home, facility, or service in which the juvenile will be placed and develop a more detailed service plan. In

some states, however, the judiciary insists on its right to specific placement of juveniles. The judge should explain the terms and reasons for the disposition decision.

At a dispositional hearing a juvenile has the right to the following:

- present evidence and subpoena witnesses

- cross-examine witnesses

- examine and dispute evidence

- have an attorney address the court

The purpose of the dispositional hearing is to give the prosecution and the juvenile a chance to ensure the court's information is accurate and to bring to the court's attention factors both parties believe are important to consider in the disposition decision.

Disposition Options

Probation

Probation is a disposition option for a juvenile court judge. A juvenile placed on probation returns to his or her community after agreeing to follow conditions set forth by the judge or probation officer. Probation usually lasts from six months to one year. After successful completion of probation, juveniles are released from the juvenile court's jurisdiction.

> Probation is clearly the most frequent disposition handed down by the juvenile court judges.... Juvenile court judges have generally adopted the philosophy that a youth will benefit more from remaining with his family or under the custody of other designated persons in the community than from incarceration (Cox & Conrad 1978).

Confinement

Another disposition alternative is confinement to a residential facility, where the juvenile will participate in programming. Programming should be designed to rehabilitate the juvenile and help ease the juvenile's reintegration into the community on release.

Aftercare involves the supervision given to juveniles for a limited period of time after their release from a residential facility. During aftercare, juveniles are still under the authority of the facility or court.

Community Placement

Juvenile court judges are more frequently using community agencies or facilities as a disposition alternative. If the juvenile poses no personal threat to the community and if a nonsecure environment would enhance his or her normal growth and development, then community placement should be considered. Two such placements are group homes and foster homes.

Group homes provide care for juveniles in a nonsecure environment. Most of the juvenile's time is spent in the community attending school, working, or participating in recreational activities.

Foster homes provide substitute family settings for juveniles. These homes offer juveniles the privacy and intimacy of family life. They provide less supervision than group homes.

Summary

Juvenile delinquency is prevented and controlled through the efforts of various sections of the juvenile justice system. The basic components of the system work together to screen, treat, and/or discipline juveniles who have committed delinquent acts.

Those juveniles who go through the screening process and pass on to other levels of the system may become involved with the police, detention facilities, juvenile court, corrections, and community agencies.

The juvenile justice system is committed to reducing the unacceptable behavior of delinquent juveniles in hopes of returning them to society as productive citizens. The system's processes and rules are geared to a younger offender in that it does not determine guilt and it does not sentence, rather, it adjudicates delinquent and gives dispositions after a hearing. The juvenile justice system is fundamentally different from the adult system so that it can more effectively deal with a fundamentally different offender.

3

Responsibilities and Training

By Lloyd Mixdorf and Rosalie Rosetti

The foundation of any juvenile justice facility or program is the careworker. The careworker is important because he or she has direct contact with juveniles placed in the facility or program and is responsible for their care, custody, and programming. Just as the careworker has many different roles to fill, the position itself may have different titles in different jurisdictions, such as juvenile correctional officer, youth counselor, juvenile supervisor, and child careworker.

The Many Roles of the Careworker

Careworkers have the difficult day-to-day job of acting as parents—caring for the large numbers of delinquent juveniles who enter the system every day. Unfortunately, careworkers cannot rely on customary parent-child relationships to do their jobs because juveniles in their care usually do not respond to customary interactions. These juveniles may come to corrections with no belief systems, shattered self-esteem, few or no social skills, and

poor academic performance. They may tend to act out and resist authority more intensely than do juveniles outside the facility.

Careworkers need to observe, listen, analyze, and decide how to relate to each juvenile in ways that will fulfill each juvenile's needs. The careworker must be responsible and compassionate. He or she must be interested in the child development process and in interacting with juveniles going through the corrections process.

In most facilities, careworkers supervise juveniles as they eat, sleep, attend school, attend programs, and recreate. Careworkers also control movement within the facility, maintain security, and at times, isolate or segregate those who are a threat to themselves or to others.

Because of this prominent position in the lives of the juveniles, careworkers are the staff most likely to notice the subtle movements—the reactions and interactions, the slight behavior changes—that can signal a juvenile's personal problems or successes. They are in the position to learn about the juveniles' families, their cultures, and their various approaches to life situations.

The careworker must be many things to the juveniles: a guardian, a good listener or counselor, a supervisor/program coordinator, and a role model. These roles overlap and are demanding in terms of time, energy, knowledge, skill, and understanding.

Lloyd Mixdorf is juvenile projects director in the American Correctional Association's Training Division.

Rosalie Rosetti is training project director in the American Correctional Association's Training Division.

Guardian

The primary responsibility of a careworker is to provide care and safety for juveniles. In the role of guardian, the careworker must ensure that each juvenile has his or her basic needs met: adequate food (three balanced and pleasantly served meals a day, plus snacks), clean and adequate clothing and linen, and clean individual rooms and general living areas. They must make sure personal hygiene routines are followed (taking showers, grooming hair, brushing teeth, etc.) and that bedtime and wake-up schedules are followed. A careworker should be aware of the juveniles' health problems and see that they receive medical or dental care when needed.

A portion of each careworker's day is devoted to basic supervision.

To ensure the personal safety of the juveniles, a careworker must control or prevent bullying or assault by others, manage aggressive behavior, and keep up-to-date on fire and emergency plans and procedures. In addition, the careworker must report all items in his or her area that need repair or maintenance to keep the physical plant safe, secure, and comfortable.

Counselor

The careworker must be an adept counselor. Juveniles detained in the facility express their anxiety in a variety of ways: extreme indifference, open hostility, or a veneer of cooperation. They range from being extremely withdrawn to being extremely aggressive. To work effectively with these troubled and troublesome juveniles, careworkers must use the interpersonal and crisis counseling skills they learned in training.

Counseling skills and role modeling work hand-in-hand. Many of the juveniles in correctional facilities have already been counseled so extensively that they know all the right answers. Many of them perceive counseling as a joke or as a putdown.

Careworkers need to treat their role as counselor carefully. Those who give too much advice and/or operate under the "do as I say, not as I do" theory are seldom successful. The careworker whose behavior is consistent and who sets a good example is the one who encourages the juvenile to trust and

to move toward habilitation. Therefore, the most critical quality of a careworker is stability. Careworkers cannot help troubled juveniles if they themselves have no stability in their lives.

Because residential juvenile facilities or programs must provide for the needs of juveniles twenty-four hours a day, it is important for careworkers on different shifts to communicate with each other about the progress of, or problems with, juveniles under their mutual care. This is usually done by recording significant happenings in a daily log book.

In their role as counselor, and in many of the other roles they fill, careworkers must be able to observe behavior objectively and to write reports on

---

The careworker whose behavior is consistent and who sets a good example encourages the juvenile to trust and to move toward habilitation.

---

what they observe in nonjudgmental, logical, clear, and concise language. Written daily logs and special incident or discipline reports can be critical in placing juveniles correctly and in meeting their needs. The careworker's ability to record events succinctly and thoroughly is crucial.

Supervisor/Program Coordinator

A relatively large portion of each careworker's day is devoted to basic supervision. Although the basic security concerns, such as being alert to possible escape attempts, searching juveniles and their rooms for contraband, and maintaining control over items that may be used as weapons, are critical, daily supervision entails much more.

It means interacting with juveniles as much as it means watching over them. Juveniles in general are often hyperactive, confused, and difficult for adults to understand. Juvenile offenders are even more difficult to manage as a result of their additional problems. A good careworker must provide structure, instruction, and guidance. Juveniles may respond appropriately to supervision when they are alone or with a few other juveniles, but they may present a different, more resistive behavior when in a group. Learning to handle large-group behavior is a critical skill for a careworker.

To ensure an effective program, juveniles need to be kept busy in productive activities at least fourteen to sixteen hours a day. Idleness is the largest contributor to depression, security, and runaway problems. Allowing juveniles to watch television and play table games for large blocks of time each day has proven to be bad treatment and poor security management.

The careworker must not only ensure that juveniles participate in their scheduled activities but must also help or lead them in the activities. For example, in the classroom, the careworker might

---

A good careworker must provide structure, instruction, and guidance.

---

serve as an assistant teacher, and during recreation, he or she might teach the juveniles the rules of a game and the value of team work.

Specialists, such as teachers, social workers, psychologists, doctors, and nurses usually provide treatment services, but the careworker is responsible for setting the tone for all other program segments. They do this by being a good role model for the juveniles, being there to listen and encourage them, helping them with their education (i.e., homework and projects), and creating positive activities for the juveniles.

In many facilities, careworkers are closely involved in education and treatment programs. Acting as teacher assistants or as craft, literacy, or recreation specialists, careworkers supplement the formal education program. After additional specialized training, careworkers may also staff group or individual counseling programs.

Role Model

Being a positive role model is probably the most important responsibility a careworker can undertake. Modeling good behavior, or setting an example, can affect juveniles in a positive manner more than any other careworker skill. Included in this activity is setting a positive tone or climate, respecting the juveniles, praising them when appropriate, being consistent and fair, and

The careworker's ability to record events succinctly and thoroughly is crucial.

presenting a generally positive attitude. Admittedly, this positive, encouraging attitude may be difficult to maintain when working with angry, rebellious juveniles, but it is absolutely necessary.

Training for the Careworker

The careworker position is entry-level and usually requires a high school or high school equivalent education. But, because of the high level of responsibility and the variety of special skills required to perform the many roles a careworker must assume, the careworker should undergo continuous special training.

Careworkers should be trained in the practical routines of the job.

Careworkers need to know and understand their agency's philosophy, mission, policies, procedures, and regulations. They must be expert in their interpersonal and counseling skills, as well as in their supervision and management skills. They must also know the limits of their responsibility and authority and understand the judicial and legislative decisions that affect what they do on the job.

Poorly trained careworkers with no prior experience can become a threat to themselves and to others.

The American Correctional Association has set a minimum standard of 120 hours of training to be provided during the first year of employment as a careworker, followed by 40 additional hours each year thereafter. Careworkers should not be expected to carry our their responsibilities before completing that minimum requirement.

ACA suggests that the following list of topics be included in the careworker's training program:

- facility's philosophy for handling troubled juveniles

- juveniles' rules and regulations

- rights and responsibilities of juveniles

- human relations and communication skills

- crisis intervention

- special needs of juveniles

- problem solving and guidance

- grievance and disciplinary procedures

- security procedures

- physical restraint procedures

- supervision of juveniles

- report writing

- significant legal issues

- interaction of the elements of the juvenile justice system

- relationships with other agencies

- fire emergency procedures

- first aid and life-sustaining functions

After completing the training program, careworkers should be able to do the following:

- gain a broader view of their job and how it relates to the total system of juvenile justice, especially the work of the courts and other public and private child care agencies in the community

- understand the psychology and the practical applications of juvenile behavior

- relate in a positive way to the behavior problems of the juveniles for whom they are responsible

Careworkers should be trained in the practical routines of the job and in the specific activities and skills required on the job, especially the skills they need to handle behavior incidents.

Training alone, however, does not make a good careworker. A healthy, positive attitude and a fundamental understanding of juvenile offenders, who are sometimes very difficult, are also essential. The ability to sort out priorities, supervise activities, and provide a balanced approach while managing a group are critical elements to good carework. Day-to-day experience is the best way to develop and perfect these skills.

Training Structures

Because juvenile facilities operate twenty-four hours a day, seven days a week, facilities use one or more of the following approaches to provide training:

- on-site, formal classroom training

- on-the-job training

- administrative staff meetings

- correspondence courses

- academy training

- outside speakers

Formal Classroom Training

The optimum training approach is on-site, formal classroom training designed with measurable objectives, varied training strategies, hands-on application, and an evaluation component. In formal training, new careworkers are given many opportunities to learn and to practice new procedures under the skilled eye of a trainer who can ensure that bad habits do not develop.

On-the-Job Training

Out of necessity, much of the training that newly hired careworkers receive takes place on the job, given by an experienced employee. Effective on-the-job training does not mean that new careworkers are simply given their assignments, told what to do, and left to do it. Just as in formal training, on-the-job training should orient the careworker to the mission and goals of the facility, and it should demonstrate the mission through daily facility practices. Veteran careworkers should model behaviors and attitudes the new worker needs to acquire.

On-the-job training is more effective when the new employee can spend time with more than one experienced staff member. By working with various staff members, the new worker can observe different approaches to handling the same problems and can adopt those with which he or she feels most comfortable.

Administrative Staff Meetings

Another effective way new careworkers are trained is through well-planned, regularly scheduled administrative staff meetings. These meetings can be used to discuss problem areas and give the new or less experienced careworker an opportunity to see how more experienced staff have handled or would have handled similar problem situations.

Short, well-written, relevant articles from journals, magazines, or books may be distributed during meetings and used as a launching pad for discussions. Although regular administrative staff meetings are not a substitute for formal training, they should be used at times to train.

Correspondence Courses

Careworkers may also be trained through a correspondence course program. Correspondence courses allow staff to learn on their own time and at their own pace. They give learners information in coherent, interrelated, and repetitive steps so that the learner can use new information as soon as he or she studies it.

Alternatives

Academy training is another alternative for careworkers. Although careworkers must leave the facility to attend classes, they have the opportunity to meet with other correctional workers from other settings to share experiences. The academy experience, however, cannot replace training given at the facility, which is specific to the operation of a pertinent program.

Summary

Although social workers, educators, nurses, psychologists, and food service and maintenance staff are necessary for a well-run facility, careworkers are the backbone of all program success. Careworkers have a very difficult job because they must be parent, teacher, coach, disciplinarian, listener, supporter, and caretaker all at the same time. New program ideas will fail in implementation without the understanding and acceptance of the careworker. Regular input from careworkers to administrators can help institutions provide the best services for juvenile needs.

APPLICABLE ACA STANDARDS

3-JTS-1-D-01–14
3-JDF-1-D-01–14

4

Rights and Responsibilities of Juveniles

By James Raymond Bell

There can be no discussion about the rights and responsibilities of detained juveniles and juvenile corrections workers without a clear understanding of *parens patriae* and the duties it imposes.

Since the first juvenile court was established in 1899, the doctrine of *parens patriae* set the agenda for the juvenile justice system and those working under its auspices. *Parens patriae* recognizes the state's authority to intervene in family matters to protect the state's interests in juveniles. The doctrine holds that to protect the state's interest, the juvenile court and its officers have the right to intervene benevolently in directing the care and custody of the state's juveniles.

Thus, juvenile corrections personnel are given tremendous authority and responsibility over the lives of juveniles. In fact, the law requires that since the state has the authority to deprive a juvenile of his or her liberty, then it has the duty and responsibility to treat or rehabilitate the juvenile before he or she becomes tomorrow's adult criminal. It is in this context that the rights and responsibilities of juveniles must be analyzed.

The Changing Nature of Juvenile Detention

Many detention facilities are crowded, and many careworkers feel that they have to provide more with fewer resources. This phenomenon is not isolated to corrections alone. Nothing in society happens in a vacuum, and juvenile corrections is facing the consequences of what is happening in society as a whole.

Every eight seconds of every school day a juvenile drops out of school. Every twenty-six seconds of every day a juvenile runs away from home. Every sixty-seven seconds a teenager gives birth. Every seven minutes a juvenile is arrested for a drug offense. More than two-and-a-half million incidents of child abuse are reported annually. More than 500,000 juveniles are held in juvenile detention facilities on any given day. (Simon et al 1991)

These statistics reflect the tragic situations of juveniles in the community. The changing face of detention brings with it juveniles who have no

---

James Raymond Bell is an attorney with the Youth Law Center in San Francisco.

values or totally inappropriate values, who use violence as a way to resolve conflicts, and who lack respect for themselves and others. Careworkers often have to deal with juveniles who are "bad, mad, sad, and can't add."

By understanding what is legally required of juveniles in detention and careworkers, the juvenile justice system's goals of treatment and rehabilitation can be met.

Juveniles' Rights to Access

The right to access for juveniles in detention refers to the right to access family and other important people in their lives. It also refers to access to the legal system. In most instances there is a right to reasonable access.

When considering access issues, it is important to keep in mind that the juveniles are confined for treatment and rehabilitation. Access to the community is critical in many cases to the ultimate success of the institutional program. Many juveniles, even those accused of violent offenses, need the emotional support of their family and friends. Thus, contact with families should be encouraged and should be limited only when it is necessary for institutional security or other appropriate reasons (e.g., the family is involved in criminal activity with the juvenile or is smuggling contraband).

Access to Visitation

For many detained juveniles, the detention experience is new and scary. Family visitation gives them a glimpse of the outside world and gives them some semblance of normalcy. The right to visitation may constitute a fundamental liberty interest under the Constitution, and therefore, significant reasons must be given when infringement of the right is considered (*Taylor v. Armontrout*, 888 F.2d 555 [8th Cir. 1989]).

Visits should be available several hours a day, with alternative visiting times provided for parents who are unable to schedule visits during normal hours. Regular visitors should include family and friends, as long as they do not threaten a documentable security interest.

Several court cases involving juveniles give the parameters of the right to visit. In *Gary W. v. Louisiana* (437 F.Supp. 1209 [E.D. La. 1976]),

More than 500,000 juveniles are held in juvenile detention facilities on any given day.

juveniles who are delinquent and mentally ill or retarded and placed in Louisiana institutions are entitled to unrestricted parental visits. The court found that such visits are important for rehabilitation and for monitoring institutional treatment. In *Thomas v. Mears* (474 F.Supp. 908, 911 [E.D. Ark. 1979]), the court ruled that there should be daily visits between juveniles and their families and attorneys at reasonable times.

Visits are often restricted because of lack of staff or space. Institutions should be careful about citing this as justification for restriction of visits. In *Ahrens*

Many juveniles, even those accused of violent offenses, need the emotional support of their family and friends.

---

v. Thomas (434 F.Supp. 873, 899 [W.D. Mo. 1977], affd. in part, rev. in part, 570 F.2d 286 [2d Cir. 1978]), the court found that inadequate facilities for visiting, with no opportunity for privacy, and limited visiting times violated the juvenile's First Amendment right to communicate with friends and relatives. Restrictions were not related to legitimate government interest, were not reasonably related to the reasons for confinement, and were greater than necessary to protect institutional security interests.

Visits with attorneys are deemed quite important by the courts. Attorneys should make reasonable requests for visits. The visits should be conducted in private, and they should not be monitored.

Access to Telephones

Court cases have not set a precedent in the absolute requirement of telephone use. A legally sound policy requires that the facility provide reasonable access to telephones. A juvenile should be allowed a minimum of two telephone calls per week that cannot be taken away for disciplinary purposes. The calls may be made to parents, other relatives, attorneys, and others. All telephone calls are subject to the institution's policy for administering telephone calls; for example, staff should dial the phone numbers to make sure victims aren't being called. Monitoring may occur only when there is justification.

Access to Mail Services

There are two categories of mail: privileged and nonprivileged. Privileged mail is mail between the juvenile and his or her attorney, a judge, a legislator, or some other public official. Privileged mail is usually designated as such on the envelope (e.g., the words "legal mail" written on the envelope). Privileged mail may not be opened by staff, except to inspect it for contraband (*Wolff v. McDonnell*, 418 U.S. 539, 574-77, 94 S.Ct. 2963 [1974]).

All other mail is considered nonprivileged mail. Mail from someone outside the facility to a juvenile may be inspected for contraband, but may be read by staff only if there is reason to believe that the mail contains escape plans, plans for criminal activity, obscene material, or material that constitutes a violation of the law (e.g., a death threat). Even then, staff must be able to articulate the reasons for suspicion before opening and reading the mail. It is not enough for them to base their suspicions and subsequent actions on a feeling or a hunch. Unless staff are able to provide factual basis to support their suspicion, they may not read the mail. They must be able to present specific information based on the juvenile's record or other facts related to institutional security.

As a practical matter, the facility should inspect mail for contraband in the presence of the juvenile or have a juvenile monitor present when the mail is inspected to prevent complaints that staff are reading the mail. Outgoing mail should be handled under similar precautions. Juveniles should be allowed to seal their mail when they give it to staff for mailing. Doing so leaves no room for argument that staff read the mail when they inspected it.

The courts are concerned about total discretion by staff regarding what mail is read or censored and what mail is left alone. Staff may read the mail only if there is a particular institutional security reason to do so. A blanket policy that allows any staff member to read mail at anytime would be considered a violation of the juveniles' rights and would be struck down as unconstitutional.

A good example of this is *Milonas v. Williams* (691 F.2d 931 [10th Cir. 1982], cert. denied, 460 U.S. 1096 [1983]). At the time this lawsuit was entered, staff at the Provo Boys School were reading all of the

---

The courts are concerned about total discretion by staff regarding what mail is read or censored and what mail is left alone.

---

juveniles' outgoing mail and judging the mail's content. The school claimed that this policy was instituted for therapeutic reasons. A letter that contained information staff felt to be untrue or a demonstration of negative thinking (e.g., criticism of the school) would be brought to the juvenile's attention; the juvenile would then be forced to rewrite the letter. Also, letters were sent out with notations written by staff in the margins (e.g., the word "manipulative" written in the margins). The court found such conduct by staff to be unconstitutional.

Access to the Courts

Juveniles have a Sixth Amendment right to reasonable access to their attorney to challenge unlawful conditions and to seek redress of their constitutional rights (*Procunier v. Martinez*, 416 U.S. 396, 419, 94 S.Ct at 1814). Juveniles also have a right to face-to-face, unmonitored visits with their attorney (*Keker v. Procunier*, 398 F.Supp. 756, 762 [E.D. Cal. 1975]).

Access to Programming

The purpose of detaining juveniles is to bring about their treatment and rehabilitation. Thus, whenever a juvenile is confined for more than a few days, there should be some kind of programming for that juvenile.

The Supreme Court has never expressly ruled on the constitutional due process right to treatment for juveniles. The Court has recognized a right to treatment for adult mentally retarded offenders, who, like juveniles, are confined for treatment without their consent (*Youngberg v. Romeo*, 457 U.S. 307 [1982]).

Access to Education

Education is the prime mode of providing programs to confined juveniles. State law requires juveniles to attend school until a certain age, and juvenile institutions must comply with state law requirements. Academic instruction may be the single most important service juvenile institutions can provide, because many juveniles in institutions are far behind in their studies or have actually dropped out of school.

Many delinquent juveniles have learning disabilities or emotional problems that have gone undetected or unaddressed by the school system. These juveniles will lag increasingly behind academically and become more alienated from the school system, unless their problems are addressed.

A significant percentage of juveniles in juvenile institutions are educationally handicapped as defined by the federal Individual with Disabilities Education Act (20 U.S.C. §§ 1401 et seq.). Institutionalized juveniles

are constitutionally entitled under this act to a state-funded and appropriate education. Under federal law, the requirements for special education are triggered when the juvenile has been confined for thirty days (*Martarella v. Kelley*, 359 F.Supp. 478,

---

Academic instruction may be the single most important service juvenile institutions can provide.

---

485 [S.D.N.Y. 1973]; *Morales v. Turman*, 364 F.Supp. 166, 174 [E.D. Tex. 1973], citations omitted, revd. 430 U.S. 988 [1977]; *Morgan v. Sproat*, 432 F.Supp. 1130 [S.D. Miss. 1977]; *Inmates of Boys Training School v. Affleck*, 346 F.Supp. 1354, 1369-70 [D.R.I. 1972]).

Most institutions lack the resources to conduct appropriate screening and identification of juveniles needing special services, and few have the resources to do an adequate job of developing individualized education plans (IEP) or implementing them. As a result many institutions have difficulty implementing the special education laws. Few institutions are able to offer the special education services required by federal law and corresponding state statutes.

Education is the prime mode of providing programs to juveniles.

In *Nick O. v. Terhune*, the plaintiff, a California resident, had been in need of special education services since he was eight years old. Even though detention in a California Youth Authority (CYA) reception center is supposed to be temporary, because of crowding, he spent more than thirty days at Northern Reception Center. The length of his stay indicated that the special education requirements should come into effect. Because the reception center was not designed to be a program institution, the juvenile's IEP was not implemented, and there was no planning for him. CYA also had long-term problems with failure to identify all juveniles in need of special education, to follow regulations for documentation of files and involvement of parents, and to provide adequate staff. CYA had been found to be out of compliance on some of these same issues in previous federal and state department of education investigations and audits.

Recreation helps the time pass more quickly for detained juveniles.

In addition to special education, juveniles have a right to a regular education. If a juvenile of school age is in detention for more than three days, the right to education is invoked. Education is a significant issue in juvenile detention. The U.S. Department of Education recently established the Office for Correctional Education at the federal level. There is a lot of action in the federal system and some state systems to put literacy requirements in place as conditions for parole. To enforce literacy requirements, institutional systems must ensure programs are in place to serve juveniles properly.

Access to Exercise and Recreation

Court cases vary greatly as guides to what exercise must be provided juveniles in detention, but as a minimum, juveniles should have an opportunity for at least an hour per day of outdoor, large-muscle exercise, weather permitting.

Not only is this important for the health and development of juveniles, but it also enables them to release tension and frustration that otherwise might result in misbehavior. Juveniles in detention often perceive time as moving very slowly, and in a confined setting, a day can seem like an eternity. Recreation and exercise help time to pass more quickly, and such activity is a constructive way to burn up youthful energy.

Exposure to fresh air is important as well. Juveniles should be allowed outdoors as often as security constraints permit.

The facility should also provide other diversions, including radio, television, games, and books to occupy the juveniles' nonprogrammed time.

Access to Religion

Access to religion is not normally a major issue with juveniles, but it occasionally becomes an issue. The basic rule is that the facility must allow religious observance. The courts have said that the religion claimed by the juvenile must be a recognized religion (cults and satanism do not qualify under this criteria). The juvenile must demonstrate that he or she is a believer in that established religion. This can usually be done by checking with the juvenile's parents or guardian. The key to the inquiry is to determine if the juvenile is sincere in his or her proclaimed religious affiliation.

Religious observances must be allowed, but they must be balanced against the institution's security needs. Long hair, for example, does not necessarily have to be allowed, even though it may be part of religious observance, because it can be used to conceal weapons or contraband.

Juveniles should not be forced to participate in religious services as part of a treatment program or methodology. Additionally, religious teachings or

---

Juveniles should not be forced to participate in religious services as part of a treatment program or methodology.

---

training of any particular religious belief should not be allowed. Juveniles who choose not to participate should be allowed to participate in alternative activities while religious services are being held.

Access to Proper Clothing

Juveniles have a right to regular laundering of underwear and outer clothing (*Inmates of Boys Training School v. Affleck*, 346 F.Supp. 1354, 1369-70 [D.R.I. 1972]). Clothing should be appropriate for the season. They should be allowed to wear clothing similar to that worn by juveniles in the community. The courts have not dealt with the banning of certain colors or styles of clothing worn in institutions, but with the appropriate security justification, such a ban would probably be upheld.

Work

Juveniles may be required to clean their rooms or living areas. However, they should not be made to do chores for the personal benefit of staff, and they should not be exploited for their labor. Juveniles are not being detained to do personal chores for the benefit of the administrator or supervisors. Such labor may be considered in violation of the federal Fair Labor Standards Act.

It is reasonable to expect juveniles to do the kind of work they would be expected to do at home or in foster care and tasks that specifically relate to the juvenile's therapy.

Crowding in Juvenile Facilities

Crowding is an important issue because it often affects the ability of juveniles to have access to their rights. It is a simple fact of juvenile corrections that crowding hurts programming.

Juvenile court cases have considered space issues, required single rooms, set limits on the number of juveniles who may be housed in a unit or group room, and required privacy for juveniles in bathroom use (*Thomas v. Mears*, 474 F.Supp. 908 [E.D. Ark. 1979]; *Ahrens v. Thomas*, 434 F.Supp. 873 [W.D. Mo. 1977], affd. in part, 570 F.2d 286 [8th Cir. 1978]; *D.B. v. Tewksbury*, 545 F.Supp. 896 [D.Or. 1982]).

If the crowding leads to violence, the juveniles' right to safety is violated. If an institution is chronically at more than 100 percent of capacity, the courts will not waive the rights of juveniles simply because the institution is crowded.

Using Restraints

Using restraints involves significant rights of juveniles in detention. It is important to distinguish between the types of restraints used: hard restraints (e.g., handcuffs) or soft restraints (leather straps that encircle the wrists or ankles). Once it is determined what type of restraint is being used, it must then be determined why the restraint is being used. Is the restraint being used for punishment or to regain control of a juvenile?

Handcuffs should be used only when transporting a juvenile so that, during transportation, the juvenile is being controlled and does not pose a danger. Handcuffs should not be used to attach a juvenile to a stationary object for disciplinary reasons. Juveniles handcuffed in such a way may hurt themselves.

If a juvenile must be restrained for disciplinary reasons, staff should use soft leather restraints, keep the restraints on only as long as absolutely necessary (i.e., only as long as the juvenile is violent or out of control), and monitor the juvenile constantly while he or she is in restraints. The use of restraints should always be approved by a supervisor. All staff should be trained in conflict resolution and crisis diffusion to reduce the need to use restraints. Restraints should never be used for the convenience of staff.

The courts have held that restraints may not be used for longer than thirty minutes without authorization of qualified professionals or

---

The use of restraints should always be approved by a supervisor.

---

institutional administrators (*Gary W. v. Louisiana*, 437 F.Supp. 1209 [E.D. La. 1976]). The need to use restraints on an out-of-control juvenile for longer that thirty minutes may indicate a medical problem. If such a problem is suspected, a medical professional should be consulted.

The courts require that when restraints are used, they should be applied so as to minimize the chance of physical discomfort or injury. Only standard restraining devices should be used.

It is important for careworkers to understand the constitutional rights involved with the use of restraints.

In *Youngberg v. Romeo* (457 U.S. 307, 102 S.Ct. 2452 [1982]), the Supreme Court ruled that liberty from bodily restraint has always been recognized as the core of the liberty protected by the due process clause. Additionally, in *Garrett v. Rader* (831 F.2d 202 [10th Cir. 1987]), the court recognized the due process right to freedom from bodily restraint in an Oklahoma case in which a juvenile died while in restraints in a state institution for the mentally retarded. The court noted that the liberty interest survives criminal conviction, incarceration, and involuntary commitment (at 204, citing *Youngberg* 457 U.S. at 314-316, 102 S.Ct. at 2457-2458).

Use of Isolation

Isolation is used in many institutions as a way to sanction behavior or to separate an out-of-control juvenile from the group until the juvenile regains control. In either case, isolation should be used for as short a time as possible to achieve the desired result.

The leading case on punitive isolation of juveniles, *Lollis v. New York State Department of Social Services* (322 F.Supp. 473 [S.D.N.Y. 1970], mod. 328 F.Supp. 1115 [S.D.N.Y. 1971]), involved a fourteen-year-old female status offender who got into a fight with another girl and was placed in isolation in a six-foot by nine-foot room for twenty-four hours a day for two weeks. The court found this isolation to be unconstitutional.

Since the ruling, standards and consent decrees have narrowed the scope of isolation somewhat, but it is not an exact science. If a juvenile is out of control, isolation should be used only until the juvenile regains control. Isolation longer than twenty-four hours should be approved by the facility director. Juveniles held in isolation for more than two hours must be seen by a counselor. There should be a progressive system of discipline that has rewards as well as sanctions (*H. C. v. Jarrard*, 786 F.2d 1080 [11th Cir. 1986]; *Milonas v. Williams*, 691 F.2d 931 [10th Cir. 1982], cert. denied, 460 U.S. 1096 [1983]; *Pena v. New York Div. for Youth*, 419 F.Supp. 203 [S.D.N.Y. 1976]; *Feliciano v. Barcelo*, 497 F.Supp. 14 [D.P.R. 1979]; *Morgan v. Sproat*, 432 F.Supp. 1130 [S.D. Miss. 1977]).

Use of Corporal Punishment

The courts have consistently condemned the use of corporal punishment on juveniles in institutions. Specifically, beatings with a thick board (*Nelson v. Heyne*, 355 F.Supp. 451 [N.D. Ind. 1972], affd. 491 F.2d. 352 [7th Cir.], cert. denied, 417 U.S. 976 [1974]); physical beatings and use of tear gas (*Morales v. Turman*, 383 F.Supp. 53 [E.D. Tex. 1974], citations omitted, remanded on rehg. 562 993 [5th Cir. 1977]); and grabbing juveniles by the hair, pulling them backwards, and flinging them against the walls (*Milonas v. Williams*, 691 F.2d 931 [10th Cir. 1982], cert. denied, 460 U.S. 1096 [1983]) have all been prohibited.

Juveniles' Rights to Due Process

As part of the institutional program, it is important that juveniles be treated fairly and that they believe they are being treated fairly. A good system of disciplinary due process can go a long way in

---

It is important that juveniles be treated fairly and that they believe they are being treated fairly.

---

creating an institutional atmosphere in which staff are respected and juveniles understand and accept the consequences when they break the rules. Due process requires that there be some form of independent fact finding before a juvenile can be deprived of his or her liberty. Careworkers should not arbitrarily put juveniles in isolation or room confinement without some form of hearing to determine if that action is fair.

The leading case on juvenile due process is *H. C. v. Jarrard* (786 F.2d 1080 [11th Cir. 1986]) wherein a juvenile was placed in isolation for seven days without written notice or an opportunity to defend himself. The boy was placed in isolation for laughing when another boy tried to flush underpants down a toilet. He was not told how long his isolation would last. When he banged on his door, staff shackled his wrists and legs to his bed for several hours and refused to say how long he would be restrained. Staff defended their actions saying that the boy was an unmanageable troublemaker and that this was a difficult time because of crowding and the presence of many difficult juveniles. The court was unconvinced and found that this treatment constituted a violation of the boy's due process rights.

The courts have found that juveniles are entitled to (1) advance written notice of the charges against them, (2) an opportunity to explain their side of the incident where permitting them to do so would not be unduly hazardous to institutional safety or correctional goals, (3) an impartial decisionmaker (e.g., not the staff member involved in the incident), (4) a written decision describing the evidence relied on and the reasons for any disciplinary action taken, and (5) a procedure for appealing the decision (e.g., to the director of the facility).

Although the law does not support a right to an attorney or legal advisor, it is good practice to allow juveniles to use any legal assistance available.

Grievance Procedures

Grievance procedures are important to juveniles because they provide a means of addressing

Court decisions have consistently upheld the rights of juveniles.

perceived injustices, thereby helping in the rehabilitative process. They are also important to institutional administrators because they provide information about abuses that may be occurring. There isn't much constitutional law specifically on grievance procedures for juveniles, but there are many cases in which various forms of grievance procedures have been approved.

The basic elements of adequate procedures are as follows:

- notice to the juvenile of the availability, purpose, and scope of the procedure

- a clear and simple procedure for the juvenile to present his or her grievance to staff

- prompt investigation of the grievance (usually within three days)

- an opportunity for the juvenile to present his or her grievance to an impartial panel

- notice to the juvenile of the panel's decision

- appropriate disciplinary sanction to staff if the grievance is found justified

- written records of the grievance, investigation, decision, and final action taken

The right to a grievance should not be controlled by staff. Procedures should be in place to ensure a supervisor is notified of all grievances filed.

Summary

It is important for careworkers to understand the legal rights of juveniles under their care. Any infringement of these rights may result in legal difficulties for the facility as well as failure to meet the juvenile justice system's goals of treatment and rehabilitation.

The juvenile's right to access to family, treatment, education, and the legal system is critical to safeguard against unfair and unsafe treatment of the juvenile while he or she is held in the facility.

Any action by staff that may be considered a violation of a juvenile's constitutional rights must be fully justified. Staff must support their actions with specific, pertinent documentation. Juveniles' rights are based on definitive court cases that have established precedence. Upholding their rights is a major responsibility of the juvenile justice system and those who work in the system.

5

Understanding Juvenile Delinquents

By Barry Glick, Ph.D., NCC

Juvenile delinquency has plagued human social order for thousands of years. Some of the earliest records of this date back to biblical times, as noted in the following:

> If a man hath a stubborn and rebellious son, that will not hearken to the voice of his father, or the voice of his mother, and though they chasten him, will not hearken unto them; then shall his father and his mother lay hold on him, and bring him out unto the elders of his city, and unto the gate of his place; and they shall say unto the elders of his city: "This our son is stubborn and rebellious, he doth not hearken to our voice; he is a glutton, and a drunkard." And all the men of his city shall stone him with stones, that he die; so shalt thou put away the evil from the midst of thee; and all Israel shall hear and fear. (Deuteronomy 21:18-21).

Barry Glick, Ph.D., NCC, associate deputy director of local services, New York State Division for Youth, is a counseling psychologist, specializing in juvenile delinquency and emotionally disturbed juveniles.

Although there is no evidence that this decree was ever implemented, it certainly set the tone for what behavior would not be tolerated and the severe consequences for children if they did not follow their parents' (and society's) rules.

The need for parents, communities, and society to understand juvenile crime and why juveniles are becoming increasingly involved with antisocial behavior led, in part, to the development of delinquency theory. As society has become more technologically advanced and complex, so have the causes and behavior of juvenile delinquency. Within the past century, psychologists and sociologists have developed several clusters of theories that speculate about the causes of juvenile delinquency.

Juveniles of the 1990s

To better understand juvenile delinquency causation theories, the nature of juveniles in the context of their environment should be explored. Juveniles of the 1990s—and perhaps of the past two decades—are growing up in a world that is hostile and aggressive, a world that devalues human life. Today's juveniles live in a world that teaches them at a young age that aggression pays. Aggression is richly rewarded; it provides immediate and effective gratification. Aggressive behavior is learned from family, peers, television, the movies, and the newspapers; it is learned in homes, schools, and communities.

According to a 1989 study conducted by the National Association against Media Violence, the average juvenile watches 27.6 hours of television per week. According to the study, during any one hour of prime-time television there are thirteen incidents of violence depicted. Many juveniles grow up watching Saturday morning cartoons. The study found that there are thirty-two acts of violence depicted per hour on Saturday mornings.

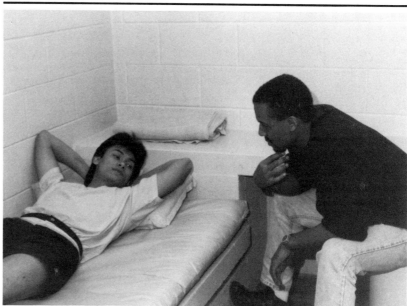

Juvenile delinquents of today often suffer from low self-esteem and feelings of hopelessness and helplessness.

Because juveniles are so desensitized to aggression and violence, juvenile arrests and crime incidents have increased by 300 percent from 1970 to 1975. The number of juveniles accused of committing violent crimes, such as robbery, aggravated assault, and homicide, has increased by over 200 percent from 1970 to 1975. According to the Federal Bureau of Investigation's

Today's juveniles live in a world that teaches them at a young age that aggression pays.

Uniform Crime Report, in 1975 juveniles made up only 20 percent of the population, but they accounted for 43 percent of the arrests. In 1978, approximately two million juveniles (under age 18) were arrested. Their crimes included larceny, burglary, vandalism, drug abuse, robbery, aggravated assault, forcible rape, and murder or manslaughter.

Schools are not immune to the problem of juvenile delinquency. Since the 1970s, schools have become beds of hostility and violence. In such conditions, students often learn that aggression

pays. Senator Birch Bayh of Indiana, in the 1975 *Safe School Report*, surveyed 750 school districts (comprising over 84,000 schools) over a three-year time span. The study indicated a drastic increase in school crimes. More recently, gang-like shootings in schools have required that metal detectors and large security forces be used in schools to curb violence.

Juveniles in the 1990s are vulnerable because there are many things that interfere with their positive development that are beyond their control. Each of the following factors deserve primary attention because their insidious nature may lead directly to juvenile delinquency.

Racism

Racism is a social plague that intrudes into the normal growth and development of juveniles. Juveniles are faced with personal racism, which involves those attitudes individuals hold and subsequent behavior they perform that are prejudicial and discriminatory. Personal racism involves name calling, bias-related violence, overt physical oppression, sexual harassment, and many other activities that affect certain classes and categories of people. The effects of personal racism on juveniles include low self-esteem, feelings of hopelessness and helplessness, and aggressive behavior that are labeled delinquent.

Juveniles should be encouraged to make a commitment to occupational or educational success and social bonds.

Institutional racism is the systematic denial of the power, privilege, and prestige available within an existing society to a group of people. Institutional racism includes the denial of access to power (social and economic), resources, and affiliation with clubs and organized groups. Institutional racism causes juveniles to group according to their own structures and often leads to the formation of gangs and other antisocial, delinquent activities.

Poverty

Poverty is so broadly oppressive that it often leads juveniles to develop attitudes of hopelessness relative to both their present and future lives. Beyond the basic needs for shelter and food, poverty limits opportunities for juveniles to participate in constructive leisure-time activities, to purchase goods and services, and to develop responsible patterns of economic behaviors. Poverty leads juveniles to develop self-effacing feelings: a lack of pride, self-worth, and esteem for self and others such that these juveniles are unable to meet their basic needs, both physical and psychological.

Cultural Acceptance

Awareness, acceptance, and pride in one's cultural heritage also lie at the foundation of a juvenile's

positive development. There is a widespread perception that "at-risk youth" are culturally deprived or culturally disadvantaged, which often leads to delinquent behaviors. Juveniles need to identify with their cultural history, roots, and role models to counteract the violence and hostility they face in their everyday lives.

Learned Aggression—The Foundation of Delinquency

Although some delinquency causation theories state that juveniles are born with the tendency to be delinquent, many theories are based on the idea that aggression is the underlying root of delinquency and that aggression is a learned behavior. Some conditions that promote aggression and lead to delinquency include the following:

- having weak familial and/or social bonding
- being a frequent target of aggression
- observing aggression used successfully
- being positively reinforced for aggressive behavior
- lacking sufficient information-processing skills and abilities
- lacking sufficient moral reasoning skills
- lacking sufficient alternative prosocial skill competencies

Theories on Delinquency

Theories on delinquency are based on the environmental and sociological factors that lead juveniles to delinquent behavior. A basic knowledge of the theoretical perspectives of delinquency will help the careworker develop a better understanding of those interventions, programs, and services designed to help delinquent juveniles.

Control Theories

Control theories assume that the inclination to perform antisocial behavior lies within the individual. As such, society is blameless, and the juvenile is considered deviant. Because antisocial, delinquent behavior is internal to the juvenile, society must assist the juvenile to control his or her internal, hostile, and rebellious behavior.

Nettler (1974) explained in his social control theory that social behavior requires socialization. Socialization as used in this context means the learning of appropriate social skills, behavior, attitudes, and values to successfully negotiate one's environment. Juveniles, therefore, will become

---

Many theories are based on the idea that aggression is the underlying root of delinquency and that aggression is a learned behavior.

---

social and acquire morals through social interaction processes. According to Nettler, unsuccessful socialization leads to nonconformity. Thus, juvenile delinquency is a consequence of unsuccessful and improper socialization. The lack of family or social bonding falls within the social control theorists' explanation of delinquency causation.

Another social control theorist, Hirschi (1969), stated that juvenile delinquency occurs when the juvenile's relationship to society is weak or broken. He suggests that the elements of the bond to society include attachment, commitment, involvement, and belief. The significant units of control in society are the family, school, and law. Juvenile delinquency, according to Hirschi, is probable when the following conditions are present:

- an inadequate social attachment on the part of the juvenile to parents and school

- an inadequate or nonexistent commitment to occupational success or educational process

- a lack of development in the moral right of the law and the belief to uphold it

Cultural Deviance Theories

Cultural deviance theories include theories that juvenile delinquency is a result of the juvenile's desire to conform to cultural values that directly conflict with those of the accepted moral and social order of conventional society. It includes all of those attitudes and values that one holds that are different from the social norm. Very often, these theories do not tolerate cultural and social differences, and as such, delinquency is the product of not conforming to accepted social values and behavior. For example, in order for a juvenile to join a gang, he or she may be asked by the gang to assault another juvenile, steal from his or her family, or deface a school wall. All of these values conform to the values of the gang, but are in direct conflict with accepted moral and social order of conventional society.

The core of cultural deviance theories attempts to integrate and address three related issues:

- the apparent concentration of juvenile delinquents within certain social strata of society or neighborhoods

- the process by which an individual within a specific geographic area comes in contact with or engages in delinquent behavior

- the process by which juveniles perform high-delinquency actions in groups and the problems that ensue when these groups menace existing cultural structures

An early proponent of cultural deviance theory was Miller. Miller (1957) stated that certain lower class cultural values are in direct conflict with the dominant middle class value system. Because much of Miller's theory was directed toward juvenile delinquent, lower class boys, he believed that juveniles who conform to lower class culture and undergo normal socialization processes "almost automatically become deviant, particularly in relation to legal standards." Miller's theory implies that these juveniles are so involved within their social culture that conventional values and law have different meanings and are irrelevant to their daily existence.

Another aspect of cultural deviance is that of the violent subculture. Wolfgang and Ferracuti (1967) defined juvenile delinquency as a "set of values, attitudes, beliefs and behavior patterns that are shared in densely populated urban areas and support the use of physical aggression and violence as an interaction form and a way to solve problems." They go on to say that this violent behavior is learned and tolerated within the lower class structure. This environment prescribes this behavior and endorses antisocial activities.

Yet, not all cultural deviance theories endorse the idea that criminal deviance is a characteristic innate to the individual. Two theories in particular reject this notion and propose that delinquent behavior is learned as an adaptation to real-world societal and cultural forces. These theories, as a subset of cultural deviance theories, place less blame on the individual as being antisocial and look more toward society as the main thrust for delinquency causation.

One theory is the differential association theory (Sutherland & Cressey 1970). This theory suggests that criminal behavior is learned behavior and derives from interactions the individual has with small groups of intimates or peers who are

---

Not all cultural deviance theories endorse the idea that criminal deviance is a characteristic innate to the individual.

---

engaged in delinquency. Juvenile delinquents learn general criminalistic attitudes and motivations, as well as specific antisocial behaviors. Such learning involves precisely the same mechanisms as learning any other type of behavior, i.e., modeling, role playing, receiving feedback on one's performance, and practicing on one's own (Goldstein & Glick 1987).

Another theory that is one step farther away from the idea that individual responsibility causes delinquency and closer to the idea that societal sources are the basis of criminal behavior is the differential opportunity theory (Cloward & Ohlin 1960). This theory proposes that criminal behavior grows from differential access to legitimate and illegitimate opportunities to reach both personal and social gains. When culturally approved means are blocked, illegitimate opportunities are sought and used. Certainly, the recent economic downturn and the increased underclass may underscore what is suggested by Cloward and Ohlin:

...the disparity between what lower class youth are led to want and what is actually available to them is the source of the major problem.... Adolescents who form delinquent subcultures ...have internalized an emphasis upon conventional goals, and unable to revise their aspirations downward, they experience immense frustration; the exploration of nonconformist alternatives may be the result. (p. 17)

Differential delinquency theory may be illustrated by juveniles who sell drugs. These juveniles may see many things they want, such as gold chains, cars, and lots of spending money, but they realize that they have no opportunities to acquire these items or to satisfy their needs. Their criminal activities arise from their differential access to purchase power (their limited legitimate access to earning money) and their access to drugs and markets to sell drugs (their illegitimate opportunities to obtain money).

Other Theories

There are a variety of other delinquency prevention theories that have at least a modest impact on understanding juvenile delinquency. Sociopolitical theories emphasize that forces outside the individual are responsible for criminal behavior. The social labeling theory (Becker 1963; Lemert 1967; Schur 1971) is one example. This theory, unlike the differential association and differential opportunity theories, focuses on society's reaction to the person. Emphasis is placed not on the transgressive or aggressive behavior of the individual, but rather on society's reaction to this behavior. Deviance is seen not as something inherent in any given behavior, but as something conferred on behavior by societal representatives.

Social labeling theorists believe that assigning a label, e.g., "juvenile delinquent," creates an expectation in both the persons themselves regarding future antisocial behavior as well as others. Over time, this self-fulfilling prophecy quality of the label or stereotype increases the actual occurrence of such behavior. The created role of the juvenile delinquent enforces a progressive commitment for that person to violate rules and deviate. Social labeling theorists believe that America's juvenile justice system creates much of the antisocial behavior it is supposed to correct. In fact, these theories teach that the further into the system a juvenile gets, the broader and more fixed the effects of being labeled.

Radical theory (Abadinsky 1979; Meier 1976) is the extreme of sociopolitical theories and is sometimes referred to as "the new criminology." Radical theories reach far beyond social labeling and focus on the political meanings and motivations underlying society's definitions of crime and crime control. Crime, according to radical theorists, is a phenomenon largely created by those who possess wealth and power (as defined by America's social structure). America's laws are the laws of the ruling elite and are used to control, dominate, and suppress the poor, minorities, and the powerless. The following specific propositions that constitute radical theory (Quinney 1974) further define its substance:

Institutional programs offered to juveniles may prevent them from further involvement in the correctional system.

1. American society is based on an advanced capitalistic society.

2. The state is organized to serve the interests of the dominant economic class—the capitalist ruling class.

3. Criminal law is an instrument of the state and ruling class to maintain and perpetuate existing social and economic order.

4. Crime control in a capitalist society is accomplished through a variety of institutions and agencies that are administered by a government elite and represent ruling class interests for the purpose of establishing domestic order.

5. The contradictions of advanced capitalism—the disjunction between existence and essence—require that the subordinate classes remain oppressed by whatever means necessary, especially through the coercion and violence of the legal system.

6. Only with the collapse of capitalist society and the creation of a new society, based on socialist principles, will there be a solution to the (juvenile) crime problem.

Indeed, in today's social action, much of the radical theorists' thinking is present in some of the social movements that have developed. These solutions to criminal activities, however, do not lend themselves to realistic implementation. Yet, social, economic, and political conditions do continue to provide a situation for juvenile delinquency to occur and a forum for these ideas to grow and flourish.

There have been other theories that have evolved during the past two decades. These theories have become popular as a result of the increase in juvenile crime, as well as the increase in aggression and violence. Many of these theories are rooted in sociological and psychological principles and are offshoots of adolescent developmental theories. Goldstein (1990) summarizes juvenile delinquency causation theories in *Delinquents on Delinquency*. In it, he gives the perspective of the true experts in this field—the delinquents themselves.

Delinquency Prevention

Although antisocial behavior must be considered part of normal juvenile development, a person who understands its causes realizes that delinquency can be prevented. The careworker needs to be aware that even juveniles who are incarcerated participate in some form of delinquency prevention. If nothing more, programs offered within juvenile correctional systems may prevent a juvenile from further involvement in the juvenile or adult justice system.

What is prevention? According to Caplan (1964), a community mental health specialist whose work has been applied to other human services areas, there are three categories of prevention:

- primary—those prevention services that attempt to reduce the number of disorders or problems of all types in the community

- secondary—those prevention services that attempt to reduce the duration of the disorder or problems

- tertiary—those prevention activities that attempt to reduce the change that may result from the disorders or problems

Bolman (1969) elaborated on Caplan's categories by defining primary prevention as attempting to prevent a disorder from occurring, secondary prevention as attempting to identify and treat at the earliest possible moment so as to reduce the length and severity of the disorders, and tertiary prevention as attempting to reduce to a minimum the degree of handicap or impairment that results from a disorder that has already occurred.

To better understand this concept, think of a man who comes home every day, takes off his shoes, and finds a hole in his sock. He proceeds to mend his sock. He does this every day for a long while before deciding to investigate further and finding a small nail in his shoe. He removes the nail and, although he does not get a hole in his sock every day, he still has to mend his sock frequently. One day he realizes that a hole left by the nail was creating the problem, so he repairs the sole of his shoe. The result is no more sock mending. Tertiary prevention may be likened to coming home and darning the sock every day, secondary prevention to removing the nail from the shoe but still having to mend the sock, and primary prevention to repairing the shoe so the sock is not damaged in the first place.

Summary

The careworker has much to contribute, once he or she understands the nature of delinquency. With a greater awareness of what causes delinquency, how it may be prevented, and what alternative strategies are available, the careworker is in a good position to foster juvenile development and habilitate the juvenile delinquent. Whether the careworker provides services in the institution or in the community, it is critical that the careworker apply his or her knowledge and experience to foster juvenile development.

Understanding juvenile delinquency, its causes and prevention, is a critical task for the careworker. The information presented here should help careworkers to interact with juveniles in their care. The juvenile is the primary client of the careworker; however, it is critical to be mindful that significant others—teachers, friends, and especially family—are also important to the success of habilitating the juvenile delinquent.

6

Behavior Management

By John Morgenthau

Physical facility design features of correctional facilities were once viewed as the primary means of behavior management. Staff's relationships with juveniles are now considered the primary source for managing behavior. Modern correctional practices emphasize the development of positive relationships between staff and juveniles.

Effective careworkers directly influence the behavior of juveniles, but they cannot control it; juveniles control their own behavior. Careworkers should use a variety of techniques to encourage juveniles to learn behavior that is social rather than destructive, aggressive, withdrawn, or otherwise inappropriate. Behavior management is about getting juveniles to learn new, appropriate behavior and to be consistent in behaving properly. Juvenile behavior management in an institution consists of helping juveniles understand what is expected of them in the correctional environment and helping them modify their behavior to meet those expectations.

Effective careworkers emphasize teaching new behavior, not punishing misbehavior. Instead of trying to control juveniles, careworkers teach self-control.

John Morgenthau is a partner in the firm of Morgenthau & Plant Associates, a national justice and corrections consulting service based in Tallahassee, Florida.

Commitments of Behavior Management

There are many effective behavior management techniques. Each careworker has his or her own way of applying techniques that reflect his or her personality. These techniques, however, should be

---

Effective careworkers directly influence the behavior of juveniles, but they cannot control it; juveniles control their own behavior.

---

based on commitments that help the careworker and juvenile establish a mutually agreeable working relationship. Careworkers should make a commitment to build good relationships with juveniles, maintain professional demeanor, teach new behavior, and think before acting.

Effective careworkers know the juveniles under their care. Juveniles should be seen as individuals, not a faceless group. Careworkers should talk with juveniles during noncrisis times, instill a sense of purpose, and provide feedback and recognition for appropriate behavior. When careworkers have good relationships with juveniles, they are more likely to

Careworkers should interact with juveniles when things are quiet.

do what a careworker requests, even if they do not agree or are afraid of losing face with other juveniles.

Careworkers must stay calm and professional in the face of irritating juvenile behavior. Juveniles will test staff at every turn to get staff to react as many adults have reacted to them in the past—with anger, distrust, or violence. Careworkers should understand that juveniles are not attacking them personally, but the adult world in general. It is easy to remain calm when one does not take criticism personally.

Careworkers should accept each juvenile as an individual capable of learning new, appropriate behavior. Instead of using punishment, effective careworkers teach problem-solving skills to help juveniles learn new behavior they can use to meet their needs in appropriate ways. Juveniles who have learned problem-solving skills have the tools to control their natural impulsiveness and disregard for consequences. Problem-solving teaches self-control. Effective careworkers model appropriate behavior.

Ineffective staff have a knee-jerk reaction to juveniles' inappropriate behavior—they look and react. Effective careworkers are more deliberate.

They try to base their response on a quick assessment of the specific juvenile, the current situation, and their own condition (for example, their own personal level of frustration or fatigue). Effective careworkers respond in a way that will be most helpful to the juvenile.

Building Relationships

When a juvenile first comes to a facility, careworkers should take time to introduce themselves. Careworkers should describe what is expected from the juvenile and what the juvenile can expect from the careworkers.

Careworkers should let juveniles know that they are expected to control their behavior and act in an acceptable manner. They should also tell juveniles that they may need to learn new behavior to avoid problems in the institution.

Juveniles should be assured that they can expect to be treated fairly and as individuals, given help in understanding the formal and informal rules of the unit, encouraged to succeed, taught new behavior, and disciplined, when necessary.

Building a relationship with a juvenile means establishing rapport, expressing a sincere interest in him or her, and developing mutual respect and

Careworkers should let juveniles know that they are expected to control their behavior and act in an acceptable manner.

trust. It does not mean being "one of the guys" or being overly easy or lenient. It does not mean blind trust.

To develop a good relationship with a juvenile, careworkers should do the following:

1. Treat juveniles with respect.

2. Show concern for juveniles as individuals.

3. Interact with juveniles when things are quiet, not only when dealing with problems.

4. Get to know the juveniles.

5. Let juveniles get to know them by discussing neutral subjects, such as favorite television shows, hobbies, or other leisure-time interests. Personal information should not be freely shared with juveniles.

6. Discuss behavior or misbehavior in behavioral terms to help juveniles identify acceptable and unacceptable behavior.

7. Help juveniles assess their behavior. Juveniles will see careworkers as a resource that can help them understand what is going on and solve their problems.

8. Review plans and expectations. Have juveniles evaluate how they are doing and provide feedback. Ask for feedback on how careworkers are doing.

Juvenile Behavior

The following are important to remember when thinking about juveniles and their behavior:

1. A juvenile's behavior is his or her best effort to satisfy one or more needs.

2. Behavior is chosen. Juveniles control their own behavior. Behavior can be influenced by others, but it cannot be controlled by others.

3. Behavior is learned. Juveniles use behavior that has worked in the past to satisfy a need.

In establishing a good relationship, careworkers should get to know what juveniles think, what bothers them, and what they like. Knowing these things helps careworkers determine the type of behavior a given juvenile is displaying and the best response to that behavior.

By carefully observing a juvenile's behavior, careworkers will usually see a pattern. Careworkers should watch for how the juveniles handle authority figures and how their peers influence them and find out to what degree they are violence-prone and whether they have a short temper. Careworkers can learn what behavior will set a juvenile off, how he or she is likely to react, and how other juveniles will react.

Also, every juvenile has a unique history. Careworkers should read juveniles' case records to become familiar with their home environment and what they have done previously to meet needs.

Alert careworkers can organize behavior they observe into one of three basic categories: approve, tolerate, or intervene. Approve behavior is

---

In establishing a good relationship, careworkers should get to know what juveniles think, what bothers them, and what they like.

---

appropriate for the facility or program. Tolerate behavior may not be quite right, but it may be acceptable in the current situation. Intervene behavior needs to be stopped.

Approve Behavior

When a juvenile does something right, he or she is doing an approve behavior. Delinquent juveniles typically have received very little teaching in appropriate behavior or praise for that behavior from adults. Therefore, approve behavior for delinquent juveniles would be considered normal, expected, or commonplace for other juveniles. Saying "thank-you," waiting for a turn, and not joining a fight are things one is expected to have learned before becoming a teenager. For delinquent juveniles, these basics stand out as approve behavior.

Delinquent juveniles learn things in small steps. Careworkers should be alert to small behavioral improvements. A juvenile may hold his or her temper just a little bit longer than the last time. He or she may do an assignment just a little faster or neater or better. Although the task may still not be successful or the final action appropriate, there is some progress.

Behavior management techniques for approve behavior emphasize giving praise or some other form of positive reinforcement. Careworkers should remember that juveniles under their care really need praise. A careworker's praise needs to be more structured than normal to have the most impact. The following are steps to structured praise:

1. Get close to the juvenile.

2. Make eye contact.

3. Say his or her name.

4. Give a pat on the back or shoulder if touching does not bother the juvenile.

5. Give a feeling statement (e.g., "I felt very proud of you when. . ."), then describe the juvenile's behavior.

6. Be enthusiastic and sincere.

Approval should generally be shown while the behavior is occurring or very soon after it so the juvenile makes a clear connection between appropriate behavior and approval. There may be times, however, when careworkers should wait to show approval, such as when doing so would embarrass a juvenile because other juveniles would make fun of him or her for "kissing up" to staff. Careworkers should also express approval in a way juveniles can appreciate and make them feel special.

Tolerate Behavior

Tolerate behavior is behavior that is irritating, but not necessarily wrong. For instance, slowness in responding to a request, finger tapping, or grumbling can be irritating. Careworkers should keep in mind that juvenile delinquents have plenty of larger problems that need attention and should let tolerate behavior pass.

Careworkers in step with what juveniles are going through will know when to tolerate certain behavior. When juveniles suffer rejection or disappointment—a court date postponement or a parent not coming for a visit—they may be frustrated and need to let off some steam. Careworkers may decide to tolerate some backtalk, normal expressions of frustration, or resistance under these circumstances.

Sometimes a juvenile's behavior simply represents an adolescent's maturity level. Careworkers should tolerate some normal juvenile behavior that shows impulsiveness or poor judgment.

Sometimes juveniles will sense when careworkers are frustrated and try to irritate them by talking out of turn, making jokes, and making deliberate mistakes. Careworkers should remain calm and simply tolerate this behavior. Once a careworker builds a positive relationship with a juvenile, such irritating behavior should stop.

The best behavior management technique for tolerate behavior is to simply ignore it. The following are steps to planned ignoring:

1. Pick a specific behavior to ignore.

2. Completely ignore the behavior. Do not mention the behavior to other juveniles, even indirectly. Do not look at the juvenile and wait with a stony silence. Do not give any facial expression of annoyance. Do not move closer to the juvenile. Focus on something else going on in the area.

3. Watch for approve behavior. If the juvenile does any approve behavior mixed in with the tolerate behavior, praise or in some way give attention to the approve behavior.

There are two things to remember when using planned ignoring. First, the juvenile's behavior usually will get worse before it gets better. Second, nearly everyone around the juvenile needs to participate for it to work. If a careworker on one shift gets upset at the juvenile's behavior, if will be harder for the careworkers on other shifts to use planned ignoring successfully. Careworkers need to coordinate planned ignoring of selected behavior.

Intervene Behavior

If a juvenile's behavior is potentially dangerous, it is intervene behavior and must be stopped immediately. The situations in which intervene behavior occurs center around four issues: (1) harm

---

Careworkers should tolerate some normal juvenile behavior that shows impulsiveness or poor judgment.

---

to self or others, (2) property damage, (3) escape, and (4) serious disruption that prevents staff from maintaining safety or order.

Some intervene behavior, such as when juveniles are hurting themselves or others or are out of control, is immediately dangerous. In these situations, some type of physical intervention (an escort or a restraint) may be required.

When a juvenile is in a crisis situation, careworkers should be aware of the degree of self-control the juvenile seems to have because it will play an important part in determining the proper response. Careworkers should only use the degree of external control absolutely necessary to return the juvenile to an acceptable level of self-control.

A crisis situation can be divided into four phases: (1) the triggering phase, (2) the escalation phase, (3) the crisis phase, and (4) the resolution phase.

The triggering phase is the beginning of a crisis. The juvenile may already be experiencing a high level of stress just by being in the program. However, an event may start to push that stress level even higher. The event may be something as simple as a food the juvenile hates being served for dinner, a postponed court date, a call from home, or teasing from another juvenile. The juvenile starts to show some signs of being upset (i.e., getting up from a chair, withdrawing from others, raising his or her voice). At this point, the juvenile is usually still under control. The careworker should stand close to the juvenile and firmly tell him or her to calm down.

During the escalation phase, the juvenile moves to the upper level of the stress tolerance limit. This occurs if the triggering event continues or the juvenile begins arguing with another juvenile or staff member. Signs of the juvenile's stress may include heavy breathing, clenched hands, flared nostrils, a loud or uneven voice; or, for juveniles who withdraw, not eating, not talking to anyone, not showering, etc. Talking with the juvenile may still be appropriate, but careworkers may also consider physically escorting the juvenile away from the situation.

When the juvenile becomes dangerously aggressive and out of control, he or she has reached the crisis phase. Verbal intervention is not effective at this point. Careworkers' options are (1) letting the juvenile work through the crisis, making sure that the juvenile and other juveniles are not hurt and property damage does not occur, or (2) physically restraining the juvenile, perhaps with the help of other staff. Careworkers should be trained in

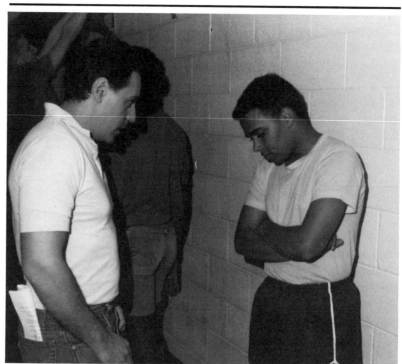

At the onset of a crisis, a careworker should stand close to the juvenile and tell him to calm down.

techniques of physical restraint before attempting to physically restrain a juvenile.

The resolution phase begins when the juvenile starts to regain some self-control. Ideally, careworkers should use the resolution phase to help the juvenile learn to handle triggering events in ways that do not lead to a crisis. Unfortunately, two

---

Careworkers should only use the degree of external control absolutely necessary to return the juvenile to an acceptable level of self-control.

---

other resolutions are more frequently used. One is to smooth over the situation by diverting the juvenile to an engaging activity, such as playing basketball or pool or watching television or encouraging him or her to "chill out." Another ineffective resolution is the power struggle. This is when the careworker and the juvenile start arguing over how the juvenile handled the crisis event. This leads to another crisis—this time directed at the careworker.

A better way to handle the resolution phase begins with the careworker being aware of the environmental factors surrounding the situation. In a crisis, other juveniles and staff are likely to be present, and they will directly or indirectly influence a careworker's interaction with the juvenile.

When assessing the environment, careworkers should consider the group's general mood, the types of relationships present among juveniles and staff, who is present, the presence of potential weapons, and the avenues available to call for help if a major disturbance develops.

Careworkers should also take time to make a self-assessment before intervening. That assessment can make the difference between a good intervention decision and a big problem. They need to remember that feelings of anger, frustration, and fear are normal. When careworkers are in situations that provoke rage, but are not prepared for the intensity of their own feelings, they will probably have great difficulty controlling their emotions and their own degree of intervention with the juvenile. When careworkers remember that these intense feelings are normal, they can move beyond them and make good decisions based on sound, professional judgment rather than poor decisions based on their own feelings and impulses.

Early Interventions

Proximity, prompting, and feedback are techniques careworkers can use in early intervention.

Proximity

Proximity is an easy, straightforward technique in behavior management that works especially well when careworkers have established a good relationship with a juvenile. When a careworker sees a juvenile starting to behave in a potentially dangerous manner, the careworker should move close to the juvenile. The careworker does not need to say anything, stare at the juvenile, or even give the juvenile a stern expression. In general, the careworker should let his or her presence do the talking. The careworker serves as a visual reminder to the juvenile to get back on track.

By using proximity, the careworker shows respect for the juvenile and teaches the juvenile how to re-establish self-control to act appropriately. If the

juvenile stops the intervene behavior, the careworker may want to give praise or some other form of positive attention.

Prompting

Prompting is a little more direct than proximity, but it is also an easy, nonconfrontive technique. Prompting means giving a juvenile a hint to stop

---

By using proximity, the careworker shows respect for the juvenile and teaches the juvenile how to re-establish self-control to act appropriately.

---

doing an intervene behavior. The goal is to be as indirect as possible, while still communicating with the juvenile. As in proximity, this approach gives juveniles an opportunity to change their behavior and to internalize what they should be doing.

Prompting may be done with hand signals, eye contact, or facial expressions. If the signals don't work, the careworker should give the juvenile a verbal hint (not a command). If the careworker needs to give a verbal hint, he or she should speak quietly, without anger.

Corrective Feedback

Corrective feedback is often used after misbehavior, when things are quiet, as a way to talk about something that has happened. It is not necessarily done in "the heat of the moment."

Feedback is an especially powerful tool in juvenile correctional programs. Many juveniles are not skilled in expressing themselves in a clear, responsible manner. They are developing new skills and need to know how they are doing. Juveniles may not be aware of the feelings of others or the effect of their actions on others. Feedback provides them critical information.

Bringing Things Back to Normal

Although an effective careworker will be able to

Communication Techniques

Basic communication techniques that aid in behavior management include nonverbal behavior, reflective listening, and receiving feedback.

Nonverbal Behavior

A careworker's nonverbal behavior may carry more meaning than words. Body language, positioning, facial and vocal expression, and eye contact ensure the careworker's spoken message is communicated clearly.

Body language helps to communicate messages nonverbally. For example, relaxed shoulders, a casual stance, and easy movements convey confidence and control. Body language may be subtle, such as tapping fingers or avoiding eye contact. These small movements may reveal that the communicator feels threatened or uncomfortable.

The careworker's physical position in relation to the juvenile is also important. Standing directly in front of the juvenile may be perceived as threatening. Instead, the careworker should stand slightly to the side of the juvenile.

Height also should be considered when communicating. Juveniles may feel threatened by a careworker who is standing over them and delivering a message while looking down. Careworkers should sit down with juveniles or get close to the same height.

Careworkers should show respect for juveniles by maintaining a comfortable distance—about an arm's length away—when communicating with them. When a careworker steps into their personal space, juveniles may feel invaded or trapped.

Facial expression conveys much of the spoken message. For example, relaxed, open facial features communicate confidence and control.

Similarly, tone of voice and volume can express more of the message than actual words. Words spoken in a warm and understanding tone can convey an entirely different message than the same words spoken in a cold or sarcastic tone. Voice volume should be kept at a normal level to maintain control and to calm the juvenile.

Careworkers can show interest in juveniles and what they are saying by maintaining eye contact. This also helps careworkers to communicate clearly and effectively.

Reflective Listening

Reflective listening is an active process in which careworkers encourage juveniles to express themselves. It helps careworkers to do the following:

- show a desire to understand the juvenile
- open the door for further communication
- establish trust and caring
- assess the juvenile and the immediate situation

Reflective listening should be used when a juvenile is calm or just beginning to get upset, while the juvenile is still responsive to those around him or her. In reflective listening, the juvenile does most of the talking. After listening to the juvenile, the careworker should describe in his or her own words what the juvenile has said. This ensures the careworker understands the juvenile and the situation.

When using reflective listening careworkers should use open and relaxed nonverbal behaviors, observe the juvenile's nonverbal behaviors, and indicate acceptance of the juvenile's feelings as real and valid.

Receiving Feedback

Feedback is an excellent tool to aid professional growth. One of the most overlooked sources of feedback for careworkers are the juveniles in their care.

To help juveniles provide useful feedback about the careworker's performance, the careworker should do the following:

1. Invite the juvenile to give feedback. Doing so opens the lines of communication.

2. Ask at the right time. This is usually right after a difficult confrontation with the juvenile and when the juvenile is alone.

3. Help clarify the message by using reflective listening skills.

4. If the feedback is negative, focus on problem-solving, not rationalizing or arguing.

avoid most confrontations with juveniles, they will occur at times. Even when confrontations are handled well, there are usually bad feelings between the juvenile and the careworker. Careworkers must work with juveniles to re-establish good working relationships.

When a confrontation is over and the juvenile has stopped the inappropriate behavior, careworkers should help the juvenile learn a new, appropriate behavior to handle the problem situation. This may be done through problem-solving or a recovery discussion.

Problem-solving

Problem-solving involves asking the juvenile a series of questions to get the juvenile to identify the problem behavior, its consequences, and its alternatives and to establish a commitment to use one of the appropriate alternatives. When things have settled down, the careworker should approach the juvenile and work through these problem-solving questions:

1. What were you doing?
2. What did you want?
3. Does that behavior get you what you want?
4. What will happen if you continue that behavior?
5. What are some other things you could do?
6. Can I count on you to try these other behavior?

These questions can help the juvenile to see the link between wants and behavior. To achieve the long-term goal of helping juveniles avoid confrontational situations in the future, it is important to spend time helping the juvenile see the link between his or her wants and behavior. Careworkers can help the juvenile identify alternative appropriate behavior to achieve the juvenile's wants.

The Recovery Discussion

After an intense verbal confrontation with a juvenile, careworkers should wait until things have settled down before meeting with the juvenile in a quiet place to have a recovery discussion.

The recovery discussion is not a counseling

session. It is a time to talk with the juvenile person to person. The following are steps for restoring a relationship with a juvenile.

1. State what took place.
2. Air feelings, thoughts, and reactions.
3. State the natural consequences.
4. State the applied or logical consequences.
5. Help the juvenile see patterns in his or her behavior.
6. Identify alternative behavior.
7. Ask for the juvenile's commitment to try a selected alternative.

The primary goal of the recovery discussion is to clear the air and re-establish a positive relationship. With these steps, however, the recovery discussion becomes a teaching opportunity. It helps the juvenile learn new behavior to use in similar situations.

Punishment and Discipline

Understanding the distinctions between punishment and discipline contributes to effective behavior management.

The Nature of Punishment

Punishment means to penalize by causing pain, loss, or suffering for a wrongdoing. Its primary purpose is to impose a consequence that results in discomfort.

An example of punishment used as a consequence would be yelling at a juvenile who has been involved in a shoving match with another juvenile. The careworker yells at the juvenile in front of the other juveniles and threatens to give a severe sanction if the juvenile doesn't get with the program. The careworker may even mock the juvenile, calling him or her stupid for acting poorly. The careworker's harsh words serve to belittle, condemn, and lower self-esteem. The careworker sends the message: "I'm in control here and I am going to punish you." Because the sanction for the misbehavior is delivered in a punishing way, the juvenile may take it as personally offensive and want to get even with the careworker.

The Nature of Discipline

Discipline is also a consequence for misbehavior. Unlike punishment, however, discipline is not intended to cause discomfort. The root word of discipline is "disciple." Disciples are learners.

Discipline is an intervention designed to teach juveniles a new way of thinking and behaving. The discipline process focuses on the following:

- ending an unacceptable behavior

- imposing a logical and related consequence for the unacceptable behavior

- helping juveniles understand why their behavior was unacceptable

- teaching new, more acceptable behavior

Discipline not only teaches juveniles what behavior to stop, it helps them understand what behavior to begin.

Discipline Instead of Punishment

The reasons for strictly limiting the use of punishment-oriented consequences in juvenile correctional and treatment programs are compelling. First and foremost, punishment does not produce long-term behavioral change. Juveniles may comply with institutional or program rules because of the threat of punishment. However, as soon as the threat is removed, they will revert to prohibited behavior that in the past has effectively met their needs. The threat of punishment has temporarily stopped them from misbehaving, but they have not learned a new, acceptable behavior to replace the existing, inappropriate one. A new way of thinking about meeting a particular need has not been internalized.

Reliance on punishment encourages artificial conformity and the repression of feelings and problems. Although it may appear on the surface that all is well, juveniles may actually be only adapting to the facility or program, just as they have adapted their behavior elsewhere to survive.

The opportunity to tap into each juvenile's potential for growth and change may be lost when punishment is used. Rather than teach new, more appropriate behavior, punishment has the unintended effect of teaching juveniles not to get caught and the value of being devious. Behavior management is reduced to a game.

Punishment also relies exclusively on external means, allowing juveniles to focus their attention on the staff administering the punishment, rather

---

Punishment has the unintended effect of teaching juveniles not to get caught and the value of being devious.

---

than actively dealing with their own behavior. It makes juveniles angry at the person who inflicts the discomfort and permits them to think primarily about getting even with the person who has wronged them.

Many juveniles in correctional and treatment programs have long, and often intense, histories of being treated in painful or negative ways, especially by adults. Punishment imposed by program staff becomes a mere continuation of the juvenile's life experience and reinforces the negative views he or she holds regarding adults in authority.

The discipline approach, which requires the juvenile to become a learner, places the responsibility for change on the juvenile. The discipline approach is more difficult to use than the punishment approach for a number of reasons:

1. Discipline takes more time and thought than punishment. Responding to each juvenile individually and relating a consequence to a specific misbehavior demands more of staff than simply enforcing a rule.

2. Discipline requires patience and kindness. The positive effects of discipline are often hard to see because most juveniles learn new behavior slowly. They may even resist attempts at discipline, preferring to be punished and not having to accept personal responsibility for misbehavior.

3. Discipline can't be forced. It can only be taught. Juveniles can resist the learning situation that is structured, and this may frustrate staff.

4. Discipline may give the appearance of not being tough, of letting juveniles get away with

misbehavior. This would be true if the program's purpose were punishment, not helping juveniles change their unacceptable behavior.

In certain circumstances, however, the use of a form of the punishment approach is warranted. The most common instance is when a juvenile presents both an immediate and ongoing threat to the safety of others. Some juveniles' internal controls are so lacking that the use of less coercive, discipline-oriented approaches is sometimes too risky. If the aggressive juvenile's behavior is chronic, however, nothing less than removal from the scheduled activity will effectively protect others and send a message to the aggressive juvenile that such assaultive behavior is unacceptable. A general rule for staff to follow is to use a discipline approach whenever a juvenile is violating rules but is maintaining personal control.

A punishment-oriented approach should be considered whenever the juvenile is losing or has lost self-control. The punishment-oriented approach does not include belittling or condemning remarks. Instead, remarks are kept to a minimum. If a physical intervention is required, it is done professionally, with a minimum of harm to the juvenile. The point is that the careworker is taking control. This is done quickly, efficiently, and with professional demeanor.

Juveniles with Special Needs

The complexities and pressures of today's society are producing a growing number of juveniles with special needs. Facilities are accepting more and more juveniles with serious problems, such as substance abuse, mental health problems, and extreme emotional instability. Some emotionally disturbed juveniles present a special problem to careworkers because the juveniles do not see the relationship between their behavior and its consequences. There is often no rational explanation for their behavior. The effectiveness of behavioral management techniques depends on the juvenile's ability to relate behavior to consequences. Therefore, juveniles with special needs are not likely to respond to these behavior management techniques and will require specialized treatment. Careworkers need to identify these juveniles early and refer them to specialized services.

Summary

Careworkers who consistently use behavior management techniques will find they make working with juveniles more pleasurable and easier. Effective careworkers generally enjoy their work. They are not unaware of the frustrations and tensions that are a part of working with juveniles, but they also experience the fun of working with them. Careworkers help juveniles get control of their lives; they experience success in forming positive, teaching relationships with juveniles and watching them learn new, appropriate behavior. They feel in control of their work. Additionally, careworkers new to behavior management techniques will find that they can get more done with less effort.

APPLICABLE ACA STANDARDS

3-JTS-3-C-01–24
3-JDF-3-C-01–21

7

Intake Administration and Classification

By Charles J. Kehoe

Intake administration and classification are the first steps in the juvenile's journey back home and can determine how successful the juvenile will be with his or her institutional experience. Every careworker assigned to these functions plays a major role in the outcome of this process.

Intake

The purpose of intake administration is to ensure the juvenile is properly admitted to the facility. Because the intake process is the first phase of a juvenile's stay in an institution, the process must be thorough, accurate, and efficient. The juvenile may find himself or herself away from home for the first time. Although the juvenile may appear to be tough and threatening, he or she may actually be fearful and depressed. It is important for the careworker to treat the new admission in a pleasant and courteous way. Showing respect for and understanding of what the juvenile is experiencing helps to prevent

Charles J. Kehoe is director of the Commonwealth of Virginia's Department of Youth and Family Services in Richmond, Virginia.

problems during admission. The careworker should take the time to explain each step of the intake process clearly before beginning.

Identification and Recording Information

The first duty of staff working in the intake unit is to confirm legal authority to admit the juvenile. In a juvenile detention facility, this step involves reviewing the petition or complaint the police officer or probation officer brings with the juvenile. In a juvenile training school, admissions staff review the authorizing document or court orders for the juvenile's name and instructions.

The next step is to collect personal information about the juvenile, such as date of birth; sex; race; parents' names, addresses, and phone numbers; height; weight; school attended; and descriptions of any identifying marks, scars, or tattoos.

Information about the offense committed is also recorded and includes the current charges, previous arrests and dispositions, and any outstanding bench warrants or court orders.

The date and time of admission are recorded, and a registered number is assigned to the juvenile. These steps represent the beginning of the juvenile's case record in the institution.

Because there is always a possibility that a facility may be sued or that an individual staff member may be accused of wrong doing, the accuracy of the information recorded at this time is critical. Case files are frequently used in court cases as evidence of how well the facility did or did not do its job.

Searches

The safety of the newly admitted juvenile, of juveniles already in the program, and of staff depends on staff being alert and attentive to details. The best way to prevent a dangerous situation is to do a thorough search of the juvenile and his or her belongings before he or she is moved from the admissions room to another location in the institution. Before conducting a search, staff should tell the juvenile what is about to happen and what will happen if a weapon or other contraband is found.

Inventory of Personal Property

Every new admission should be patted down immediately on arrival. An itemized list should be made of the juvenile's property on a property record form. The process is completed in the presence of the juvenile, and the juvenile signs and dates the form indicating that it is an accurate description of his or her property. The careworker countersigns and dates the form. The juvenile is given a copy of the signed form, and the original is kept in the case file. All property should be kept in a locked area. Money and other valuables should be stored in the institution's safe or other secure location.

The juvenile may keep personal property as defined by facility policy. Such items may include legal documents, family photographs, glasses, hearing aids, dentures, address books, and correspondence.

After the juvenile's identification and case information have been recorded, he or she may be escorted to the shower area by a staff member of the same sex as the juvenile. The juvenile should be instructed to disrobe. All personal clothing and belongings should be searched, and a record should be made of the date, time, and place where a weapon or other contraband is found. The weapon or contraband should then be placed in a proper container, identified, and turned over to the appropriate authorities as prescribed by institutional policy and state law.

Intake is the first phase of a juvenile's stay in an institution and should be conducted thoroughly and efficiently.

In juvenile detention centers, weapons, contraband, or clothing may be evidence in the criminal act that led to the juvenile's detention. If the careworker has reason to suspect that the clothing or personal property of the juvenile is evidence, the careworker should contact the chief administrator immediately.

During the showering process, the careworker should look for signs of physical abuse, tatoos, marks, injuries, or substance abuse. A record should be made of any findings. If abuse or mistreatment is apparent or suspected, the chief administrator should be notified immediately so that the appropriate referrals will be made, consistent with state law and institutional policy.

Issue of Personal Items

After the shower, the juvenile is issued personal property. The personal property includes clothing, sneakers, toiletry articles, and bedding. Each of these items should be recorded on the appropriate form and signed for by the juvenile. The record should be kept in the juvenile's case file.

Photographing and Fingerprinting

As permitted by state law and institution policy, the juvenile is photographed and fingerprinted during the admission process. The photos are used for identification at the time of release and in the event of an escape. Fingerprints are kept on file for identification as well.

Health Care Screening

Health care screening is a process of observation and inquiry that is used to prevent juveniles who are a safety or health risk to themselves or others from being placed in the facility's general population. Health care screening also identifies juveniles who need to be transported to health care facilities immediately.

Health care screening may be conducted by health care personnel or by a careworker trained in health care. The information obtained is recorded on a form approved by the health care administrator.

Health care screening covers any medical, dental, and mental health problems the juvenile may be having or has had in the past. Substance abuse screening may also be done at this time.

The juvenile should be observed carefully to determine state of consciousness, mental attitude, general appearance, conduct, and signs of physical distress, such as tremors or sweating. New admissions are frequently depressed or angry. They fear parental rejection, punishment, and isolation. In some cases they may be overwhelmed by guilt. Thoughts of suicide may be very much on their mind. Suicide may seem like the only alternative. The juvenile's behavior must be reported in detail. Any unusual behavior should be reported to the appropriate administrator immediately. All staff should be trained to handle potentially suicidal juveniles.

In some cases, juveniles arrive at a detention center under the influence of drugs or alcohol. If a juvenile must undergo detoxification treatment, the treatment should be administered at a community health facility *prior to admission* to the detention facility. When treatment is administered in the facility, it must be done under the close supervision of medical personnel and trained facility staff.

Following the health care screening, program staff should be informed of the juvenile's medical problems or physical problems that may require medical attention. Proper notification is made in the daily log or other log as required by facility policy.

Each facility should have procedures for screening and isolating new admissions who display symptoms of contagious diseases or where such conditions are indicated in the juvenile's

---

All staff should be trained to handle potentially suicidal juveniles.

---

medical history. Procedures ordinarily require admissions staff to immediately notify the medical personnel that a possible problem exists and to arrange for the transportation of the juvenile to the appropriate health care facility.

During the health care screening, juveniles are also told how they can access sick call help.

Notifying the Family

During the admission process the juvenile should be allowed to make at least two local or collect long distance telephone calls to family members, an attorney, or other approved individuals.

In addition, the facility should inform parents or guardians, by telephone, of the juvenile's location, visiting hours, and directions to the facility. The telephone call should be followed with a letter that confirms the telephone conversation and includes the facility rules regarding mail, telephone calls, and visiting.

Temporary Classification and Assignment to a Housing Unit

Based on information delivered with the juvenile and on information from the intake interview with the juvenile, intake staff will decide the juvenile's immediate and temporary classification based on his or her needs, risk level, history of assaultive behavior, history of escape attempts, and special needs, including the need for protection. Assignment to a housing unit is based on the juvenile's temporary classification. A more formal classification is made following the assessment and evaluation period.

Special Needs Juveniles

Juveniles with special needs include the following:

- those who are mentally retarded, mentally ill, or emotionally disturbed
- those who have substance abuse problems
- those who require protective custody
- those in need of special medical attention
- those who present security problems
- those who are suicidal
- those who are extremely violent

In these cases, intake processing can require extra staff, additional time, possible use of restraints, special supervision, and security precautions.

Careworkers assigned to special needs juveniles have additional training that enables them to better help these juveniles.

Orientation

Orientation is the means by which a newly admitted juvenile is informed about the facility—its programs, rules, and expectations. Orientation is usually started following the initial intake procedures.

An orientation handbook explains the facility, what will happen to the juvenile while he or she is there, how the juvenile can access facility programs and services, and the rules that must be followed. Each juvenile is given his or her own copy of the handbook. If a juvenile does not understand English, a translation

---

Orientation is the means by which a newly admitted juvenile is informed about the facility—its programs, rules, and expectations.

---

of the handbook is provided in the juvenile's language. If literacy is a problem, a staff member assists the juvenile in understanding the material.

Orientation also includes formal and informal classes, group discussions, distribution of written materials regarding juvenile rights and grievance procedures, and sending orientation materials to parents.

Observation of the juvenile's behavior and interaction with other juveniles also takes place during orientation.

Completion of orientation is documented by a statement signed by the juvenile and countersigned by the appropriate staff member.

Intake Programming

The process of intake administration and classification is a demanding one. Most juveniles will be spending their time during the day in orientation, interviews, psychological testing, health and dental appraisals, educational evaluations, groups discussing programs and services, and other admissions-related activities.

Newly admitted juveniles should be provided regular programming to the extent possible. They should be permitted to participate in educational programs, recreational activities, receive exercise, attend religious services, and perform work assignments on their units. They should also be provided reading materials.

Idleness and boredom can be serious problems during this period. The use of volunteers can help maintain an active schedule for the newly admitted juvenile.

Classification

Classification is the process used to determine the treatment and security needs of committed juveniles and to assign them to facilities and programs based on their needs, the level of security required, and the availability of resources.

Classification can take place at a designated reception and diagnostic center, in a juvenile court probation department or juvenile detention facility, or at the reception unit in a larger facility.

The purposes of classification are (1) to evaluate a juvenile's behavior and background to determine his or her treatment and security needs, (2) to develop an individual treatment plan, and (3) to

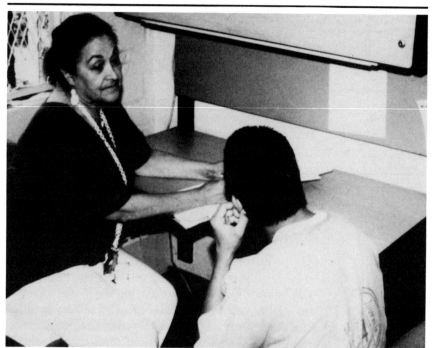
During intake, juveniles spend most of their time in interviews with staff.

Classification also helps the administration to manage facilities and resources and to develop specific programs based on the needs of juveniles committed to the facility.

In some states, the classification team will conduct the necessary evaluations and tests and analyze the background material. Then, based on the team members' professional judgments, they will develop an individual treatment plan, including identifying the facility where the juvenile is to be transferred.

With technology, however, more objective ways are being developed that have the classification team reviewing a predetermined risk and needs assessment and restrictiveness scale that will help to identify the type of programming the juvenile needs and the level of security.

review the program and status of each juvenile at least once every month.

Classification Process

The juvenile's treatment plan is developed by a classification team. Team members are usually specialists concerned with evaluating, testing, and looking for causes of a juvenile's behavior so a program can be developed that will help the juvenile avoid that behavior in the future. These individuals usually include an assistant superintendent for programs, a psychologist, a counselor or social worker, a teacher, a vocational teacher, a nurse, and a careworker supervisor.

The classification team is responsible for analyzing the information available on the juvenile from a social history (also called a dispositional report), school records, police records, medical histories, psychological and psychiatric exams, vocational tests, religious backgrounds, and interviews with the juvenile and his or her parents.

Proper classification ensures juveniles are assigned to the least restrictive placement consistent with public safety. Juveniles should not be placed in programs that are more secure than their security level requires.

Individual Treatment Plan

The classification committee designs a personalized program for and with the juvenile that states expected goals and behavior. The plan identifies objectives and time frames to be achieved, specific

---

Proper classification ensures juveniles are assigned to the least restrictive placement consistent with public safety.

---

plans for meeting the objectives, necessary institutional and community resources, and specialized services. Persons responsible for implementing the program and the evaluation methods are also included. The expected accomplishments must be measurable and agreed on by the juvenile and the staff.

The entire plan must be reviewed monthly and revised when needed. This review ensures the juvenile is not overlooked in the system and allowed to linger unproductively. Monthly reviews must be documented in writing to ensure compliance by the facility's team.

Appeal Process

Decisions that change the classification of a juvenile can have a significant impact on the juvenile's liberty, access to services, conditions of confinement, and eligibility for release. Due process safeguards that ensure a level of appeal above the classification team should be available to the juvenile whenever there is a change in classification.

Classifying Juveniles with Special Needs

Juveniles with special needs as identified earlier need to be classified and identified by types of behaviors, numbers of juveniles, and frequency of commitment. When the frequency of commitment can justify the need, programs should be started for the appropriate management and treatment of these juveniles.

APPLICABLE ACA STANDARDS

3-JTS-5A–5B
3-JDF-5A

8

Programs and Related Services

By The Information Advisory Committee
Kentucky Department of Social Services, Division of Children's Residential Services

Facilities for juvenile offenders in America are being transformed from those that meet only the basic needs of juveniles to those with programs that focus on treatment and rehabilitation. Today's society is faced with an aging population and cannot afford to think of juveniles as disposable. Greater efforts to make juvenile offenders productive members of society are critical.

Juvenile correctional facilities today are much more than places to warehouse young offenders. Innovative programming has become an integral part of the juvenile facility landscape. Programming helps in management of the facility and orderly control and security within the institution.

Decisions about programming must be based on the needs of the juvenile population. Typically, juvenile offenders are educationally and emotionally unprepared to function effectively in society. They have poor social and interpersonal skills. These needs and more must be addressed to facilitate personal change in the juvenile offender.

The Information Advisory Committee coordinates data, articles, and reports generated from the Division of Children's Residential Services, Kentucky Department of Social Services.

Counseling Services

An important aspect of treating juveniles within a residential setting is the counseling services they and their families receive. Counseling must focus

Programming helps in management of the facility and orderly control and security within the institution.

not only on the juvenile's identified problems but also on those of the juvenile's family situation. Individual, group, and family counseling services should be provided.

Initially the individual sessions focus on helping the juvenile identify what changes he or she needs and is willing to make. Subsequent individual counseling sessions focus on setting up a plan to achieve these changes. The plan is based on short-term achievable goals and objectives. Individual sessions may focus on the juvenile's strengths and resources, barriers he or she perceives may be encountered, and ways to overcome these barriers.

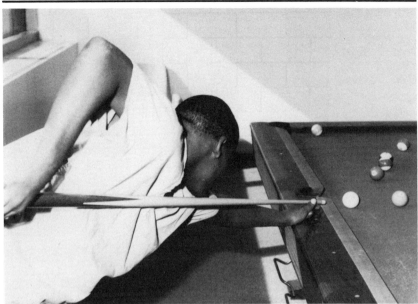
Programming helps in management of the facility and orderly control and security within the institution.

These services are provided by psychiatrists, psychologists, social workers/juvenile counselors, and trained paraprofessionals who receive the appropriate training and ongoing supervision. The effectiveness of counseling is enhanced by regular communication between the counselor and the careworker responsible for supervising the juvenile about issues being dealt with in counseling.

Careworkers can reinforce the goals and objectives of counseling while supervising daily activities. They can give invaluable feedback to the counselor and juvenile regarding improvements or deficiencies the juvenile may display during the daily routine. This feedback can be material for future counseling sessions. It is imperative that the various staff components within a facility work as a team.

Group counseling, which for many years has been a valued method of treating juveniles within a residential setting, uses the juvenile's own peer group to create change within the juvenile's behavior, attitude, and value system. It also offers juveniles a source of support and encouragement from their peers.

Family involvement in the treatment program is critical because the majority of the juveniles will eventually return home. Family counseling can be used as a way to better understand the problems presented by the juvenile and those encountered by the family. Adapting the method used in individual counseling, a plan would be developed with family members to achieve the changes they are seeking.

The juvenile justice system has become more sophisticated in addressing the specific treatment needs of juveniles through specialized treatment components. These components may include sexual offender treatment, drug and alcohol treatment, expressive therapies, and aggression replacement training.

Implementation of these components into the treatment program will vary from facility to facility. Sometimes they are incorporated into the daily counseling routines or implemented at specific times or days during the week. They may often be accessed only through community resources.

Education

The education program in juvenile facilities helps to ensure success for juveniles when they are released. There appears to be a direct relationship between

---

Family involvement in the treatment program is critical because the majority of the juveniles will eventually return home.

---

poor academic performance and delinquency. Research indicates that very few juveniles re-enter school and complete requirements for a high school diploma after being in a juvenile facility (Buchard & Buchard 1987). A quality education program is critical.

Juveniles enter correctional facilities at various times throughout the year. The academic profiles of these juveniles vary from nonreaders to college-level functioning. Their lack of interest in school is evident in their ability to evade the school setting for long periods of time.

Juvenile facilities range in size from large facilities with 100 to more than 1,000 juveniles to small facilities with only 10 to 100 juveniles. Each

---

The education program in juvenile facilities helps to ensure success for juveniles when they are released.

---

setting needs a unique plan. A small setting is ideal for meeting individual treatment needs, but it cannot offer the variety of educational levels, subjects, and options needed for diverse abilities and requirements.

It is important to also consider all state and federal regulatory requirements for educating juveniles. A juvenile facility must abide by the laws and regulations designed to educate juveniles of the state in which the facility is located.

Ideally, all juveniles should be required to participate in the education program even if they had received legal permission to drop out of school prior to being placed in the facility. The facility's school program should follow the same time or length of school day required for all juveniles in that state.

Individualized instruction planning is necessary with an educationally diverse population. This instruction plan is best based on a comprehensive academic assessment rather than on school or verbal records that indicate grade level and report card grades. Many juvenile offenders in correctional facilities have been in special education programs or are in need of special education services. The provision of such services requires specific due process procedures.

An individual education plan (IEP) is helpful for all juveniles because each has a specific level of achievement and ability. The IEP is required and has specific components and development procedures for juveniles identified to be in need of special education services. Sample IEP formats and special education procedures should be available from the state department of education or from a local school district.

When beginning or restructuring an education program, it is helpful to design outcome statements of goals juveniles will strive to achieve. Staffing patterns, schedules, purchase of instructional materials, staff development, and a system of recognition and rewards should be designed to accomplish the desired outcomes.

The components of a juvenile education program will vary, depending on the educational outcomes desired and the resources available. Based on the needs of the individual juvenile, the components could consist of assessment, basic academic and survival skills, completion of high school diploma or general equivalency diploma (GED) requirements, postsecondary, specialty areas, vocational education, and work experience.

Assessment

After a week of program orientation and adjustment, an individualized academic assessment should be administered. A screening test may help to determine whether a more in-depth assessment is needed. For juveniles reading above the fifth- or sixth-grade level, the Test of Adult Basic Education may be administered. If it is suspected that the juvenile has a learning disability, the specific assessment procedures required by the state department of education should be followed. An academic assessment, used for juveniles with serious educational problems is the Woodcock Johnson PsychoEducational Battery. The results of the assessment and interviews with juveniles are used to develop the IEP.

Basic Academics and Survival Skills

Juveniles with serious academic deficiencies need program emphasis on developmental reading, writing, math, study skills, and life survival skills. Reading is an area in need of emphasis in all juvenile facilities.

Completing Diploma Requirements

Juveniles who read above a sixth-grade level and have a poor chance to complete requirements for a high school diploma may have an individualized general equivalency diploma (GED) program of study. If a juvenile is only a few credits short of earning a diploma, specific tutoring or a correspondence course system would be appropriate.

Postsecondary

Juveniles who have already earned a GED or high school diploma should still be required to attend the facility's school program. Postsecondary program options include the following:

- vocational training
- college courses—correspondence or in-class
- computer literacy
- peer tutoring
- planned work experience

Educational Specialty Areas

Depending on the needs of the specific juvenile group and the resources available for instruction, the following specialty areas may be appropriate:

- computer training
- study skills
- literature/literacy
- information skills
- decision making
- family life skills/sex education/parenting
- employability skills
- social skills
- drug and alcohol education
- moral reasoning
- independent living skills
- fine arts programs
- physical and health education

Vocational Training

The primary goal of vocational education is to, first, assist the juvenile in making career choices and, second, to develop attitudes, skills, and knowledge for entry-level employment. Effective tools for vocational training include thorough vocational assessments, career counseling, prevocational training, and competency-based job training.

Juveniles over the age of fourteen may be effectively assessed for vocational aptitude, interests, and values. An individual vocational plan should reflect the assessment information, any special needs, and specific vocational goals and objectives.

Using the assessment results, juveniles are encouraged to develop plans to pursue short-term job choices and/or long-term career choices on release from the facility. Career counseling enables juveniles to have a better concept of their talents and to become more focused on possible areas for fulfilling work.

Through pre-employability training the juvenile should readily identify personal traits that would make him or her more employable. The juvenile should understand the importance of self-marketing

---

Using the assessment results, juveniles are encouraged to develop plans to pursue short-term job choices and/or long-term career choices on release from the facility.

---

through applications and the interviewing process. Communication and goal-setting skills should help the juvenile obtain appropriate jobs.

Vocational offerings should reflect the local or state job market. Training should be provided by certified teachers. The *Dictionary of Occupational Titles* may help guide competency-based planning and vocational program completion. Juveniles should be geared toward postsecondary vocational education on release and should receive credit for secondary training obtained in the facility. In many cases, entry-level employment is also obtainable.

Work Experience

The mission of an in-house work experience program is to enhance vocational training with organized work experiences. Juveniles learn work skills and positive work habits and are able to earn money/privileges.

The process of pairing juveniles with work supervisors enables the work supervisor to function as a role model. This relationship can have a long-term, positive effect on juveniles. The program should be geared toward instruction and teaching rather than work output.

The program should be designed to recognize and reward good job performances and healthy work attitudes. By working the maximum hours per week and receiving a good rating on the job, juvenile employees will quickly advance through the four work levels: (1) entry, (2) apprentice, (3) journeyman, and (4) contractor. Juveniles should receive higher pay with each level achieved and eventually preferred contract jobs, which are established by the facility staff.

Successful advancement through the work experience program will promote basic employable skills and prepare juveniles for favorable work experiences in their home communities. Those juveniles who have reached the final level of contractor will have also earned the respect due an outstanding employee.

Employability Skills

Statistics indicate that the highest rates of unemployment have consistently been among teens and young adults (Bowers 1979). Many factors contribute to this situation, one being the juvenile's general education and the other his or her education relating to the world of work.

Juveniles served in juvenile treatment programs are often academically disadvantaged: they perform below grade level and lack reading, writing, and math skills. They tend to drop out of school because their families move frequently or because they get into trouble and have to quit. They are often fired from jobs because of irresponsible work behavior.

The term "employability skills" is one of several (others being survival skills, job search skills, school-to-work skills, etc.) that has been coined to refer to those skills necessary for successful employment search and retention. When doing job placement with juveniles, many employers say that good work habits and attitudes are more important to them when hiring than specific job skills. Employers feel they can train juveniles on the job in the skills necessary to perform a specific work task if the juvenile has the following attributes: punctuality, honesty, dependability, initiative, loyalty, the ability to follow rules and regulations, the ability to work cooperatively with others, and the ability to accept supervision.

Any employability skills training should include skills that are necessary to a successful transition from school to work, including, but not limited to, job search skills (locating job openings and application and interviewing skills) and job retention skills (adjusting to a new job, traits of a good employee, asking for a raise, terminating employment, etc.)

The following topic areas should be included in an

Computer training may be part of effective educational and vocational programs.

employability skills training program:

- finding a job
- understanding a paycheck
- understanding taxes
- keeping a job
- occupational safety
- self-appraisal for employment

When providing employability skills training it is important to use an active instructional format. This may include such techniques as role playing and videotaping job interviews, role playing a variety of workplace scenarios, completing actual job

---

Process of pairing juveniles with work supervisors enables the work supervisor to function as a role model.

---

application forms, and using a telephone to practice setting up interviews and to thank the interviewer following a meeting. The juvenile should also be taught how to use newspapers and telephone books from their community to obtain information about jobs and job-training options.

Skills learned in employability skills training may be used in other areas. For example, appropriate job interview techniques and grooming standards are also applicable to interviews with school counselors and interviews for college entrance.

Employability skills training can be most effective when coupled with a work experience program (within the facility) or work release program (community job placement) because this can reinforce good work retention habits and provide further evaluation of a juvenile's strengths and weaknesses on the job.

Independent Living Skills

In recent years there has been a lot of emphasis on providing training in independent living skills to

juveniles placed in correctional facilities. This training is also referred to as life skills, survival skills, and life adjustment skills.

Most training in independent living begins at an early age in the family unit and continues throughout development. These family experiences are supplemented by school and social experiences. However, most juveniles in correctional facilities have not learned even the most basic life skills. Therefore, when teaching independent living skills, it is important not to make assumptions about what the juvenile already knows.

There are many educational materials available to teach independent living skills; however, many of them involve reading textbooks and completing workbooks. Because of the diversity of academic functioning levels within a juvenile treatment facility, the textbook and workbook format is not effective. Many of these skills are performance skills, and they should be taught in an active format.

The variety of materials and curricula available for teaching independent living skills frequently include the following topics:

- telephone skills
- survival reading
- money skills
- transportation skills
- menu planning
- cooking and serving skills
- home and yard maintenance
- community resources
- housing skills
- personal development
- developing self-esteem
- decision making

The extent of training depends on many variables, including the amount of time available, whether training is held daily or weekly, whether training is held during or after the school program, and the length of the juvenile's stay in the facility. Many of these skills are taught in the daily routine of the facility in activities such as bed making, bathroom and kitchen clean-up, lawn and yard maintenance, and cooking. The skills can be expanded to include additional basic information; for example, cooking can be expanded to include information on nutrition, menu planning, and safe storage of foods.

Instructors for independent living skills should involve all facility staff by identifying and using the job skills, talents, and expertise of each individual. Teaching these skills can be motivating and enjoyable for staff members and, more important, can be seen by juveniles as a useful skill or knowledge to possess.

Numerous community resources are available to enhance this training. Representatives from utility companies, banks, and social and health services providers are often willing to come to the facility to make a presentation. Tours can be arranged for groups of juveniles who are authorized to leave the facility, and brochures and other printed information can often be obtained for classroom use at little or no cost. Other community resources, such as the local county cooperative extension offices, chambers of commerce, and public libraries, can provide interesting and current materials to aid in the instruction of independent living skills.

The success of this program is determined by the enthusiasm and creativity of the instructor and can become the training most requested by juveniles as they begin to see it as having the most practical effect on their lives in the community.

Recreational Services

A quality recreation program is a critical component of a juvenile correctional facility. A recreation program in any size facility needs to be organized, varied, balanced, challenging, and above all, fun. A full-time recreation specialist may be used to plan and implement the recreation program. However, in many institutions, careworkers plan and implement the recreation program. These staff, because of their close relationships with juveniles, should know the juveniles' recreational needs.

Many agencies use volunteers for specific activities, such as teaching and supervising dancing; other agencies incorporate volunteers in the entire recreation program. Volunteers are often well-liked by the juveniles because they are not drawing

paychecks and so are perceived as being there because they truly care about kids.

Another staffing resource is a university. Many universities are willing to establish a juvenile institution as a practicum site for their students majoring in physical education or recreation. This type of arrangement can benefit both parties. Being a practicum site can also provide the agency with a resource pool for future employees.

Overall, availability of recreational facilities and equipment dictates major recreational programming. Some juvenile institutions have major facilities, such as a gymnasium, a swimming

---

A recreation program in any size facility needs to be organized, varied, balanced, challenging, and above all, fun.

---

pool, ball fields, and tennis courts, on the grounds. For these institutions, recreational programming should not be difficult. Other institutions may have only one multipurpose room in which to conduct a craft class. In these cases, creativity is the key.

Keeping in mind security issues, the use of community resources should be explored. The local parks department and local school system can be valuable resources because they have numerous recreational facilities that are available for outside agency use. State parks can be used for camping programs, outdoor education, and day use. Some community resources charge a users' fee. When funds are not available, bartering with services is an alternative. The juvenile facility can offer various services performed by juveniles in exchange for the use of the facilities. Some typical services include lawn care, litter pickup, general housekeeping, painting, and general maintenance.

Each juvenile institution should have basic recreational equipment. These include, but are not limited to, age-appropriate board games, cards, basketball and goal, playground balls, softball equipment, footballs, arts and crafts and hobby supplies, and weight equipment.

A quality recreation program is based on the needs and desires of the juvenile population. Programming is the most vital aspect of a quality recreation program when dealing with juveniles. Their needs are quite simple and concrete. Their desires are much more difficult to assess because everyone is different in what they like and do not like. A recreation specialist should survey the juvenile population frequently to get ideas on programming.

Juveniles need to be outside as much as possible in the fresh air working their gross and fine motor skills. Sports help to develop motor skills and eye-hand coordination skills. Sports also provide the opportunity to teach the mental and emotional skills of sportsmanship.

Providing competitive sports is a standard in most juvenile facilities. Juveniles love to compete. Competition is good for them and prepares them for challenges they will meet when they are returned to the community. However, competitive sports, whether it be team or individual, should not be the sole focus of the recreation program. Many juveniles in correctional facilities have not been exposed to or have not been successful at team-oriented activities. Some lack even basic coordination skills. It is up to the recreation specialist to know the population and center programming around this knowledge. For juveniles to have fun during recreation, they need to have some successes.

Juveniles also want to be challenged and to take risks. For most juveniles, the more daring an activity is, the more fun it is. A recreation specialist can provide appropriate risk-taking activities. The recreation specialist should always keep in mind and be aware of safety. Some excellent programs used by many juvenile institutions are adventure-based programs: rope climbing courses, white-water rafting, camping, rock-climbing, and similar high-adventure activities.

Working in a juvenile correctional facility can be very demanding, stressful, and frustrating. Living in one can be

even worse. That is why the recreation specialist and his or her programming are so important in the lives of juveniles.

Religious Services

Most administrators in the juvenile field understand the importance of religious programs in juvenile facilities. American Correctional Association standards emphasize that juveniles have the right to voluntary exercise of their religious beliefs when those practices do not interfere with the order and security of the facility.

In most facilities, either a full-time chaplain or a representative of a faith group from the community should be available to provide regular religious services. The chaplain or religious program

Juveniles should have access to religious services.

coordinator should see that volunteer religious groups from the community have access to the population when requested. Juveniles should be kept informed about opportunities to participate in religious programs on a continuing basis.

Careworkers must be sensitive to the increase in the number of less traditional religions. Many careworkers have not had the experience of dealing with some religions that are less well-known. Nevertheless, the right of a Muslim juvenile to have

---

Careworkers must be sensitive to the increase in the number of less traditional religions.

---

a *kufi* (a particular type of headpiece) is just as well established as that of a Jewish juvenile to have a *yarmulke* or a Baptist to have the Bible. The right of a Native American to worship in a sweat lodge is becoming just as well-recognized as that of a Catholic to attend mass. Juvenile agencies are dealing with more of these situations every day, and it is the agency's responsibility to make clear the policy on how these groups are permitted to worship.

Community Involvement

Community involvement can take many different forms. It could be visiting nursing homes, preschools, or day care centers; helping to pick up litter on highways; helping out around recreational parks; helping the community to put on special events; or cleaning and painting school grounds.

There are many ways to get juveniles involved in helping their community. Involvement will help juveniles feel a sense of pride in what they are doing for their own community. They will get positive feedback when others see the results of their work, and this will make them feel better not only about their own community but, more important, about themselves. The community in turn will see the juveniles in a positive light.

Another positive outcome of community involvement can be in building relationships. This can be accomplished in either day care or nursing homes. Juveniles can get some good feelings about themselves by becoming involved with other people of different ages. Community involvement can build a person's sense of self-worth.

Summary

Today's juvenile correctional facilities recognize the importance of quality programming to aid in management of the facility and in control and security. Programming should be based on the needs of juveniles in the facility. Through quality programming, time spent in the institution can be used to help juveniles develop a secure emotional base and skills they need to function in the community.

APPLICABLE ACA STANDARDS
3-JTS-5D–5G
3-JDF-5B–5F

9

Working with Special Needs Juveniles

By Ronald L. Stepanik, Robert E. Morris, M.D., and Charles J. Baker, M.D.

Although most juveniles in correctional facilities have some unique and critical problems exclusively related to the events leading up to their law violation and resulting incarceration, juveniles identified by corrections as having special needs are those who have particularly varied and extreme problems. In addition to offense-related problems, special needs juveniles have problems that require additional support or services from facility staff, aftercare staff, and staff from other departments (e.g., psychological services and psychiatric services). Special needs juveniles have special anomalies and needs that go beyond their delinquent acts.

Ronald L. Stepanik is director of Juvenile Services for Eckerd Family Youth Alternatives in Florida.

Robert E. Morris, M.D., is assistant clinical professor of pediatrics for the University of California, Los Angeles, and senior physician, Central Juvenile Hall, Juvenile Court Health Services, Los Angeles County.

Charles J. Baker, M.D., is medical director, Juvenile Court Health Services, and clinical instructor in pediatrics for the University of Southern California.

Being Aware of a Juvenile's Special Needs

Not all staff need to know all the details of a juvenile's special needs, but most do need to know some basic information about a juvenile's condition and needs. Careworkers may need to be aware of these to help evaluate and verify the juvenile's condition, refer the juvenile to the proper specialist (i.e., clinical or medical staff), and ensure the safety of the juvenile, other juveniles, and staff.

Evaluation and Verification

When juveniles who are already identified with a special need (e.g., mentally retarded) come into the living unit, staff are often called on to observe, record, and document behaviors as part of the overall diagnostic and classification process. This process is especially critical in terms of juveniles with special needs interacting with other juveniles in a residential atmosphere. Documentation of specific behaviors when evaluating the juvenile and verifying his or her condition is invaluable to the overall diagnostic process.

Referral

Juveniles with special needs frequently fall through the cracks of the system and are not properly and quickly diagnosed. Trained and alert staff must make referrals to clinical and medical departments to facilitate the proper diagnostic and identification process. For example, if a careworker observes that a new admission doesn't mix well with the others, keeps to himself or herself, stares at the ceiling, and won't eat, the careworker should document these observations and process a referral to clinical staff.

Safety

Staff need to know as much as possible about special needs juveniles to react and respond quickly and effectively to various situations. They need to know that a particular juvenile is an extreme suicide risk and is not to be left alone, that a particular juvenile is prone to become physically aggressive and should be closely monitored, that a particular juvenile suffers from pyromania and has already set two fires in the facility, and so on.

Juveniles Adjudicated Dependent

Juveniles adjudicated dependent may well be society's best example of "throwaway children." Not only are these juveniles found to be delinquent for committing a crime, but they are also designated wards of the court, leaving them largely dependent on the legal system to meet their basic needs (e.g., food, shelter, and support).

Many of these juveniles enter the legal system at a young age. They may be designated wards of the court for various reasons, including abandonment, death of one or both parents, the failure of multiple foster home placements, homelessness, and legal removal from the custody of parents or guardians who physically or sexually abused, neglected, or otherwise mistreated the juvenile.

Those adjudicated dependent usually feel emotionally abandoned and believe adults cannot be trusted to meet their needs. They live under abnormal conditions and, as a result, have a higher tolerance of aberrant behavior. They often cannot recognize abuse because it is commonplace to them, and therefore they often set themselves up for victimization, or just as often, they victimize others.

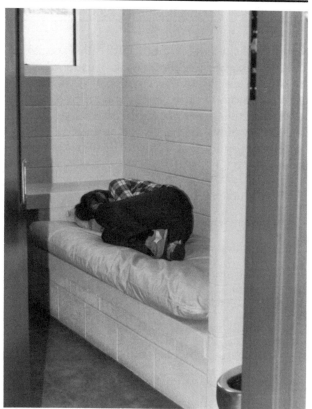

Special needs juveniles have problems that require additional support services.

Juvenile Sex Offenders

Juvenile sex offenders have committed serious crimes against others in the form of illegal sexual expression at the expense of another person. The scope of offenses committed by the juvenile sex offender is broad and ranges from molesting young children to aggravated rape.

Staff must closely supervise juvenile sex offenders while they are in treatment. This includes supervising showers, maintaining juveniles in properly assigned areas, and ensuring juveniles do not wander off alone and unsupervised.

Staff must be trained to deal with manipulative behavior and even sexual overtures from juveniles. Manipulative and sexually aggressive behavior should be documented and reported to supervisory personnel immediately. Staff must be able to deal with their own emotions regarding sexuality and at the same time remain professional and unbiased in dealing with the juvenile sex offender.

Educational Deficiencies

Exceptional student education (also called special education) serves juveniles who have extraordinary educational, social, and/or emotional needs. These programs provide varied content and methods to serve a juvenile's special needs. Terminology to describe juveniles' special educational needs continues to evolve in this field. The terms include the following:

- educable mentally handicapped
- trainable mentally handicapped
- profoundly mentally handicapped
- physically impaired
- hearing impaired
- visually impaired
- speech and language impaired
- emotionally handicapped
- severely emotionally disturbed
- specific learning disability
- gifted
- deaf
- blind

Careworkers need to know about a juvenile's special needs to best help the juvenile and to not confuse a learning disability with something far different, like purposeful disrespect.

Drug Abuse and Addiction

Many juvenile delinquents use legal and illegal mind altering drugs. They may experiment occasionally or use the drugs continuously, incurring serious psychological and physical damage. Drug addiction refers to continuing uncontrolled drug use despite serious adverse consequences. The use of some physically addicting drugs results in physical sickness or even death on sudden withdrawal. The abuse of some other drugs results in psychological addiction with severe mental distress during withdrawal but no threat to the life of the drug abuser except for possible suicidal impulses.

Underlying physical addiction is a process in which the brain makes actual chemical changes in response to continued drug use. If the drug is stopped, an imbalance results that can cause seizures or other adverse events. Psychological addiction (habituation) comes from the addict substituting and preferring the drug euphoria over normal, daily activities. The addict becomes dependent on the drug to the exclusion of other activities. Eventually, some addicts begin to experience unpleasant side effects from the drug or become aware of how dependent they are on it. At these times the addict may successfully enter treatment. Unfortunately, many addicts who end up in correctional institutions are not yet motivated to quit, and they make poor candidates for drug rehabilitation. Nonetheless, detention does separate the drug abuser from his or her drugs, which is the first step in any drug rehabilitation program. Corrections programs that take advantage of this first step may successfully rehabilitate some abusers.

Many drugs are abused. Currently crack cocaine leads the list of infamous abused drugs, however marijuana and alcohol are probably used more frequently. Abuse of narcotics and depressants

---

Detention does separate the drug abuser from his or her drugs, which is the first step in any drug rehabilitation.

(barbiturates and valium) is less common but results in physical withdrawal. Speed (amphetamines) and hallucinogens (such as LSD and PCP) are less commonly used, but are gaining in popularity, especially in certain groups. Most drug abusers combine drugs and often mix them with alcohol. Drug abusers often crave drugs, and will commit crimes to pay for drugs. Many of these drug abusers will eventually be arrested for a crime, and many will be on a drug when they are placed in detention.

Symptoms of Drug Abuse

A juvenile who is acting crazy is more likely to be on drugs rather than be mentally ill. Each drug produces its own variety of reactions. Cocaine causes a feeling of well-being in a talkative, excited, restless juvenile who will crash and become depressed a short time later. Amphetamines cause similar feelings, but are longer lasting. Narcotics and barbiturates cause slurred speech, staggering, incoordination, sleepiness, and in overdoses, decreased breathing and even death from profound depression of body functions. PCP can cause a mild dissociative reaction or severe agitation and aggression. Similarly, LSD can result in pleasant hallucinations one time and severe, uncomfortable reactions the next time. Marijuana produces few outwardly observable effects, except bloodshot eyes and a tendency to relate strange thoughts. Cocaine and amphetamines may cause dilated pupils. Some narcotics cause pinpoint pupils, and others dilate the eye.

Intravenous drug users often have permanent marks from scarring within their veins from repeatedly injecting caustic materials. This mainlining of drugs results in mainline tracks. Other addicts inject just under the skin, "skin popping," which results in puncture wounds and scars. Tatoos sometimes conceal needle scars.

Juveniles arriving in detention who appear to be under the influence of a drug should be evaluated by medical personnel before admission. Some drug reactions will suddenly progress to life-threatening events. Sometimes drug dealers swallow their products to avoid being apprehended with the drug in their possession. Several minutes to hours later, the person will experience an overdose of the drug. Unfortunately, the word of the newly detained juvenile cannot be trusted because of fear and misunderstanding. Therefore, if there is any suspicion of drug ingestion or intoxication, the careworker should notify a supervisor and the juvenile should be sent to a well-equipped emergency unit for monitoring.

If drug abuse while in detention is suspected, the unit supervisor should be notified and established procedures followed. Juveniles under the influence of some drugs, such as PCP, are very dangerous, and care should be taken in approaching them. Many of the commonly administered prescription drugs used by physicians to calm belligerent juveniles cannot be used if drug abuse is suspected because of potentially fatal drug interactions between the abused and prescription drug.

The stress of life in an institution can make a juvenile feel overwhelmed.

Treatment of Drug Withdrawal

Juveniles withdrawing from drugs are uncomfortable at best and in danger of dying at worst. Withdrawal can be treated successfully over a period of several days by a physician using nonnarcotic drugs that block the symptoms of withdrawal. It is important to notify a supervisor and to refer juveniles suspected of being in withdrawal to medical care.

The Nature of Abused Drugs

True narcotics can be divided into opium derivatives with strong sedative and addicting potential and intense physical craving, which results in severe physical symptoms if the drug is not administered regularly. Synthetic narcotics, such as Demoral, cause addiction but have a more excitatory effect. Codeine addiction occurs, but is less intense. Withdrawal of narcotics results in shivering, goose bumps, rapid heart beat, muscle and bone pain, intestinal cramping, and vomiting. These symptoms begin about six hours after the last dose and last for several days. Methadone withdrawal starts later and lasts longer.

Depressants (such as barbiturates, valium, and other sleeping pills) affect brain and muscle control. Discontinuing the drug causes various degrees of anxiety, insomnia, tremors, delirium, convulsions, and even death.

The opposite of sedative drugs are the stimulants, such as amphetamines, like benzedrine, dexadrine, methamphetamine, preluden, ritalin, cocaine, and many others. Users of these drugs are overexcited, irritable, restless, and sometimes psychotic-acting. Out-of-control behavior, as well as criminal activity, such as robbery or prostitution to obtain money to pay for drugs, often leads to the abuser's arrest. Withdrawal causes depression, apathy, days of sleeping, and disorientation. Some of these abusers will be malnourished because the drugs depress appetite, and the addict does not eat.

Hallucinogens (such as LSD and PCP) cause illusions, hallucinations, and poor perception of time and distance. PCP-induced violent psychotic episodes can require large numbers of staff and use of restraints to control the individual. Complicating this

---

Juveniles arriving in detention who appear to be under the influence of a drug should be evaluated by medical personnel before admission.

---

intoxication are serious and even life-threatening physical reactions, such as muscle damage and kidney failure. Although withdrawal signs are absent, hallucinogens do cause flashbacks during which the person experiences the effect of the drug long after (days to years) it was taken.

All institution staff must be aware that a drug overdose is potentially fatal. Any juvenile found unconscious or with altered consciousness must

receive immediate medical attention aimed at reversing the effects of the drug.

Alcoholism

Alcohol is the preferred drug for most juveniles. Many juveniles regularly consume five or more drinks on a single occasion (Mann et al 1985; Morgan, Wingand, & Felice 1984; National Institute of Drug Abuse 1990). Many delinquent juveniles report getting drunk several times each week (Mann et al 1985). Violent crimes, including assaults and vehicular manslaughter, are often committed while under the influence of alcohol.

Alcohol can cause serious liver and brain damage in adults, but this usually takes years to develop. Likewise, withdrawal symptoms occur in adult drinkers. Of more concern for juveniles is alcohol poisoning, which can lead to death from respiratory paralysis. Careworkers should inquire into the role that alcohol played in the crimes of the juveniles under their care. Appropriate referral for alcohol abuse treatment must be made for successful rehabilitation of delinquents.

Suicidal Tendencies

Suicide is the cause of death for many juveniles each year. The stress of incarceration, remorse over the crime, feelings of hopelessness, and parental abandonment all can cause a detained juvenile to consider suicide. Any mention of suicide should be taken seriously. In addition, careworkers should question their wards about suicidal thoughts whenever depression is detected. Explicit questions should be asked: "Are you thinking about killing yourself?" "Do you want to hurt yourself?"

Supervisors should be alerted if a juvenile indicates suicidal thoughts or engages in suicidal actions. The juvenile should be placed under constant supervision until a mental health or medical provider cancels the watch. A psychological referral should be made. Potentially lethal objects, such as belts, shoelaces, and sharp objects, should be removed. Even apparently normal juveniles should be observed frequently (approximately every fifteen minutes) to detect any unexpected suicide attempts. Some institutions place juveniles accused of certain crimes (such as, murder, sexual abuse, or assault on a parent) on close watch because experience has shown that these juveniles have a high risk of suicide in the first few days after they commit one of these crimes. Careworkers should be aware of events that may cause juveniles to be depressed (e.g., court rulings, parent's failure to visit, or letters of rejection).

Preventive interventions for suicide include the following:

- screening potentially high-risk juveniles

- increasing supervision

- watching for signs of depression, isolation, or distress

- listening closely to what a juvenile says

- observing changes in eating and sleeping habits

- observing neglect of personal appearance

- noting psychosomatic complaints

- observing a decline in performance of school work

- observing extreme personality change

Indications that a juvenile is suicidal include the following:

- running away

- violent acting out

- death of a relative, friend, or pet

- pregnancy or abortion

- divorce of parents or siblings

- remarriage of parent or sibling

In correctional settings, the following situations are especially critical to monitor:

- at the point of admission or early on in the juvenile's stay

- immediately after an escape attempt or major disruption

- after a disappointment (e.g., failure to pass a review, receiving a "Dear John" letter, after a pass to go home is cancelled)

- when a juvenile is placed in isolation or is under room restriction

In the case of a suicide attempt when only one staff member is supervising juveniles, the staff member should summon help before attending to the juvenile in distress. Calling for help is especially important in secure areas where the suicide attempt could actually be feigned to facilitate an escape or to cause a disturbance.

The careworker has a responsibility to do everything possible to reduce the possibility a juvenile will commit suicide. On the other hand, staff must understand that some suicides will occur regardless of all safeguards instituted and that it is

---

Staff must understand that some suicides will occur regardless of all safeguards instituted and that it is not their fault.

---

not their fault. The careworker's best tools to respond appropriately to suicide attempts are accurate information, quality training, and practice.

Mental Health Issues

Many juvenile delinquents have histories of child abuse and sexual abuse. Others experienced poverty, family deaths, murders, suicides, and other manifestations of unstable upbringing. Some have been raised in foster homes or institutions and have been moved frequently from one place to another. The juvenile may have suffered many past injuries, especially to the head, because of his or her impulsive behavior or from inflicted trauma. Parents debilitated by drugs and alcohol are unable to adequately raise children. And some parents may suffer from psychiatric diseases that have an inherited component. This means that some juveniles have both a genetic tendency toward mental illness as well as a mentally ill parent whose behavior may affect the juvenile's psychological adjustment. Combinations of these factors may lead to various mental illnesses in detained juveniles.

Neuroses and Psychoses

Mental illness takes many forms. Neurotics are generally unhappy individuals who barely cope with daily living. They experience worry, anxiety, and disappointment. Neurotics may also worry about intrusive thoughts about committing actions that they see as bad or unacceptable. Depression

---

Some juveniles have both a genetic tendency toward mental illness as well as a mentally ill parent whose behavior may affect the juvenile's psychological adjustment.

---

may result from all the worries of a neurotic. Depression leads to sleep disturbances, slow talking and moving, a depressed appearance, and decreased appetite. Phobics fear specific places or people or events. Hypochondriacs experience false illnesses and worry excessively about their health. Compulsive disorders lead to repetitive thoughts and actions.

Psychotics are unable to function in the world because they are unable to appreciate reality. They may act crazy and be aggressive or they may sit immobile for hours. Some psychotics hallucinate, especially hearing voices that often communicate unwelcome messages. A psychotic's speech rambles and often makes no sense. The psychotic makes up new words or uses words in unintelligible ways. The psychotic's emotional reactions are severely exaggerated or distorted; he or she can suffer from great despair or experience great ecstasy, sometimes shifting back and forth from one emotion to the other. In one form of psychosis, manic depression, the individual swings from deep depression to uncontrolled manic behavior during which great plans are made and much money may be spent. This type of out-of-control behavior can result in criminal conduct, such as fraud and writing bad checks. Juveniles who exhibit odd behavior or who seem to be out of touch with reality should be referred for a psychiatric evaluation.

Personality Disorders

Individuals with personality disorders do not adjust well to life and use a variety of unhealthy mechanisms to cope. They may use drugs, drink excessively, steal, or fight when stressed. They have low thresholds for frustration and act impulsively. Their ability to work and adjust to institutional life is erratic and unstable. When confronted with poor performance, they will blame something outside themselves.

Antisocial individuals take incredible risks and commit outlandish acts that persons not suffering from this disorder would never consider. Because antisocial persons do not consider the consequences of their actions, they may injure or jeopardize others. Antisocial individuals include pathologic liars, who, even if confronted with evidence of the lie, just shrug and ignore the obvious.

Many antisocial individuals have pleasing personalities and can manipulate others into helping them or even into loving them. This trait makes them very dangerous because the careworker may inadvertently be manipulated into helping a juvenile in ways that are not in the best interest of the juvenile. For this reason, institutions have rules concerning staff contact with juveniles that are meant to protect the unwary from actions they will regret later.

Personality Trait Disturbances

Individuals with personality trait disturbances engage in behaviors that tend to cause them problems with other people. Two common types of personality trait disturbances are emotionally unstable and passive-aggressive personalities.

The unstable personality looses control easily when stressed. They may panic in emergencies or respond with explosive tempers when challenged. They cannot cope with daily difficulties. Poor judgment leads to inappropriate choices and failure to establish lasting relationships.

There are three types of passive-aggressive personalities: passive-dependent, passive-aggressive, and aggressive.

Passive-dependent individuals act helpless in their dealings with others. They do not make their own decisions and seek advice for even the simplest situations. The passive-dependent person clings to institutions, agencies, or individuals for emotional support and decision making. At first a careworker may be flattered by the attention of a dependent juvenile, but soon the constant need for reassurance wears thin and the careworker may begin to become resentful.

Passive-aggressive individuals are unable to express aggression directly. They appear unable to understand directions, and they follow the literal meaning of instructions, even when it is obvious some modification is needed. Advanced planning to provide consistent, firm guidance may work with these individuals.

Aggressive individuals act out their irritations, grudges, and destructive wishes. Underneath the hostility lies deep-seated dependency. Their hostility may be verbal (lies or gossip) or physical

---

Many antisocial individuals have pleasing personalities and can manipulate others into helping them or even into loving them.

(physical attacks). Because they lack internal controls, external control must be applied to contain outbursts. The careworker can attempt to teach these juveniles acceptable outlets for aggressive impulses, such as hard work and recreation.

Passive-aggressive personalities tend to alienate others, which leads to their being ostracized. The empathetic careworker should provide firm guidance, being sure to praise good behavior as well as to discipline bad conduct.

Other Personality Disturbances

Some individuals have had difficulty adjusting since infancy. The inability to deal with daily problems is deeply ingrained, making supervised living a necessity.

Although some individuals appear to have normal intelligence, they are not able to cope with the environment. The lack of determination and advanced planning leaves them on the lowest social and financial strata. Poor judgment leads to institutionalization. Poor self-esteem allows them to accept institutional life because it makes few demands.

Cyclothymic personalities swing from depression to exaggerated feelings of well being. During the "high" periods, they are engaging, but often overreach themselves. Legal difficulties may result from this, leading to arrest. These individuals can be confusing because they seem so happy one day and bitter and depressed the next. Medication can be very helpful for some of these individuals.

Schizoid personalities shun society, preferring to be alone and unassertive. Emotional involvement with others is rare, and they appear to be isolated. They are rejecting rather than being rejected.

Paranoid individuals harbor suspicions about the intentions and motives of others. Internally, these persons may have strong negative feelings, such as envy, jealousy, and hostility, which they project onto those around them. They expect the worst because they subconsciously feel deep resentment toward most people. Individuals with these attributes cause great problems in institutions because they seize on every action to complain that they are being ill used. These vindictive, grudge-bearing individuals are unpopular and dangerous to both staff and other juveniles. The paranoid juvenile is truly frightened and believes that he or she is being persecuted. Within detention facilities there is sometimes violence among juveniles. Therefore, some juveniles will have real reason to fear. Careworkers must be diligent in separating the real dangers from the delusional.

Dealing with the Mentally Ill

Mentally ill juveniles may not be obvious at first. However, with close observation, their unusual behaviors will become apparent. Careworkers may be tempted to blame these unusual behaviors on malingering or willful stubbornness. The careworker must not ridicule the juvenile who displays signs of mental illness. This reaction will increase the juvenile's sense of isolation and lack of understanding. Likewise, other juveniles should be prevented from teasing their peer. Observing juveniles when they think they are alone will help separate malingering from mental illness.

Stages of Mental Deterioration

Previously healthy individuals may become mentally ill at any time. As their illness worsens, symptoms also become more severe. At first the juvenile may become withdrawn and seem to take less interest in the world. Later, the juvenile may refuse to follow direction, neglect personal appearance, and refuse to talk. Sleep disturbances, including sleeplessness or early waking, may begin. The juvenile may repeatedly be sent to isolation because of rule violations or violent behavior. A psychotic juvenile may experience frightening hallucinations. The juvenile may begin to hear voices and may respond to the voices. The careworker should watch for signs of mental illness before it reaches such a severe state. Being aware of the early signs of mental illness allows early intervention and improves the ultimate prognosis.

The Mentally Retarded

The term mentally retarded covers a wide range of intellectual disturbances. At the mild end of the spectrum there is only slight impairment of specific functions, such as seeing letters reversed or inability to carry out some math functions. These individuals may be referred to as learning disabled. With appropriate education these individuals can learn and lead a normal life. Juvenile institutions have reported having as many as 80 percent of their population functioning below grade level. Some of this is the result of learning disabilities and some of it is caused by lack of school attendance. What ever

Group therapy often provides effective, inexpensive care to a large number of juveniles.

the reason, delinquency has a high association with school failure.

More severely retarded persons cannot learn and do not profit from experience. They may not read or

---

Being aware of the early signs of mental illness allows early intervention and improves the ultimate prognosis.

---

do math, but they can speak and carry on a conversation. It may not be obvious that they are intellectually impaired. Because these individuals are suggestible, they can sometimes be led into criminal activity that they do not understand.

Mentally retarded juveniles need protection from other juveniles who might prey on them for sex or out of cruelty. Directions should be given slowly, in easily understood words, and one step at a time. If a careworker suspects a juvenile may be retarded, the juvenile should be referred for testing.

Medication and Treatment

Treatment of mental health problems takes many forms. Some problems can be treated in several different ways—in some cases, if one treatment fails another can be tried. Mental health practitioners and medical staff will evaluate the juvenile and prescribe the most useful and practical therapy given the available resources of the institution.

Group therapy, especially for abused and drug addicted juveniles, often provides effective, inexpensive care to a large number of juveniles. Attending Alcoholics Anonymous or Cocaine Anonymous meetings provides a link to outside programs that the juvenile can use on release.

Medication provides relief of many symptoms especially for psychotic juveniles. Because these drugs have been misused in the past, some jurisdictions now require a court order to administer psychotropic (mind altering) drugs. In emergency situations these drugs may be administered with court notification at a later date. Some powerful antipsychotic drugs may have unpleasant side effects, including muscle spasms, unusual behaviors, fainting, intolerance to heat, and dry mouth. Any juvenile on psychotropic drugs who complains of problems should be referred for medical evaluation. If the problem is serious, such as muscle spasm, the juvenile should be seen immediately because serious, even life-threatening, complications can ensue.

There are many different kinds of mental health personnel. A psychologist has either a master's degree or a doctorate degree and specializes in treating individuals with emotional or mental disturbances. A psychiatrist has a medical degree and four or more years of training in dealing with emotional diseases. The psychiatrist prescribes drugs; the psychologist does not. Social workers with masters degrees often provide counseling for individuals with mental health problems, but may refer more difficult cases to psychologists or psychiatrists. Medical doctors, such as pediatricians and internists, often have some psychiatric training and can care for some mental health problems. These physicians are also equipped to deal with the side effects of some psychiatric medications.

Mental illness can be subtle. Careworkers should be alert for the symptoms of mental illness and refer the juvenile for evaluation. Communicating with medical and psychological personnel regarding the behaviors observed on the unit provides valuable information needed to diagnose and treat the juvenile's mental illness.

Summary

Careworkers need to be keenly aware of the special needs juveniles bring with them to the correctional setting. They need to know the fundamental ways to effectively deal with special needs juveniles in concert with unit, shift, and facility rules and regulations.

Careworkers are not responsible for treating the juveniles' special needs, but are very much responsible for (1) being knowledgeable about special needs and observing and documenting specific behaviors, (2) making referrals to clinical staff as needed, and (3) doing all that is possible to ensure the safety of the juveniles entrusted to their care. Clearly, careworkers play a critical role with juveniles because they work so closely with them. The careworkers' observations and input to clinical staff are invaluable in terms of proper diagnosis, treatment, and indicated follow-up.

APPLICABLE ACA STANDARDS
3-JTS-5B-07

10

Health Care for Juveniles in Correctional Institutions

By Robert E. Morris, M.D., and Charles J. Baker, M.D.

When juveniles are confined to correctional institutions, their parents can no longer provide them with health care. Government agencies responsible for confined juveniles assume the obligation to provide medical, dental, and mental health care to their wards. Each institution must maintain medical and mental health services that, in cooperation with the institution's staff, aim to prevent serious illnesses and accidents in the institution's population.

If an institution fails in its duty to provide adequate health care, this failure may be considered cruel and unusual punishment and can result in a constitutional violation. On the other hand, negligence (medical malpractice) or a disagreement between a juvenile or the juvenile's parents and the physician concerning treatment does not constitute cruel and unusual punishment. Nonetheless,

negligence and malpractice are to be avoided to ensure the welfare of juveniles, as well as to avoid legal actions against the institution and its medical personnel.

American Correctional Association standards provide guidance on how a good institutional

---

If an institution fails in its duty to provide adequate health care, this failure may be considered cruel and unusual punishment and can result in a constitutional violation.

---

health care system should be developed and maintained. The standards require institutions to designate a health care authority to be responsible for all health care services. These responsibilities should be well defined. The authority may be an individual, such as an administrator or a physician, or it may be an agency, either governmental or private. If the authority is not a physician, final medical judgments must be made by a designated physician from some other source.

Robert E. Morris, M.D., is assistant clinical professor of pediatrics for the University of California, Los Angeles, and senior physician, Central Juvenile Hall, Juvenile Court Health Services, Los Angeles County.

Charles J. Baker, M.D., is medical director, Juvenile Court Health Services, and clinical instructor in pediatrics for the University of Southern California.

Decisions regarding medical care and access to medical care must be left up to trained medical personnel. Careworkers must be careful not to interfere with a juvenile's access to medical care. In fact, because of the immaturity of many juveniles, it is especially important for careworkers to be alert for illness that juveniles may not report.

Each institution must have an adequately equipped medical facility to provide care at the level the institution has elected to provide. Facilities can range from a simple dispensary to an elaborate hospital ward complete with operating rooms. If the institution elects to have a modest facility, then procedures must be in place to quickly transport sick and injured juveniles to an outside medical facility. Likewise, very small institutions may have no medical staff at all and will need to send all sick juveniles to outside medical facilities for care.

The medical unit should include an area where juveniles can be examined and treated in private. The size of the facility and the type of equipment used in the facility will vary, depending on the size of the institution and the extent of services to be provided. Maintenance of equipment, including periodic testing, must be done by appropriate medical personnel. Security personnel are responsible for maintaining physical security of the medical unit and its equipment.

Juveniles' Responses to Health Care

Because of their developmental stage, juveniles often exhibit contradictory behavior. A juvenile will demand independence in one breath and whine for attention in the next. These apparently conflicting communications often confuse adults who work with juveniles. Juveniles may exhibit some recurring behavior that may interfere with the delivery of health care. Even the most hardened juvenile may show fear at the thought of receiving an injection or

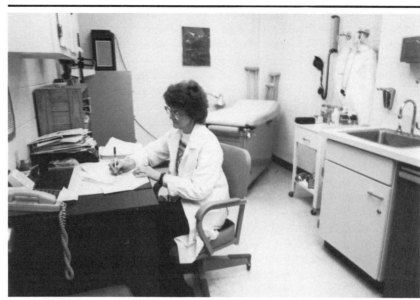

An institution's medical facility should be designed and equipped to provide health care at a level suitable to the institution's size and resources.

other health care procedure. Careworkers must avoid teasing or belittling the juvenile who is afraid. Instead, a careworker should ask the juvenile about his or her concerns regarding the procedure. Often the juvenile has an unexpected concern that once

---

Decisions regarding medical care and access to medical care must be left up to trained medical personnel.

---

discovered is easy to allay. Juveniles often process information literally, for this reason careworkers should refrain from making jokes about medical procedures. Statements such as, "If you keep complaining about your toe the doctor is going to cut it off" can cause apprehension and behavior problems the next time the juvenile comes to see a physician. Rumors about medical atrocities abound in institutions, and alert staff should stop the rumors before they become established facts in the minds of the juveniles.

Medical staff may ask careworkers or counselors for help with a reluctant juvenile. Calm discussion with the juvenile often works to uncover any misunderstandings on the juvenile's part. If the careworker or counselor is unclear about the type of procedure the juvenile is concerned about or the reason it is needed, he or she should discuss it with the health care provider before talking to the juvenile.

Trust in the doctor-patient relationship is paramount to an effective interaction between the two individuals. Juveniles confined in institutions have many reasons not to trust the institution's physicians. One reason is the juvenile's lack of freedom to obtain a physician of his or her own choosing. In addition, the juvenile may perceive the physician as having conflicts of interest and loyalty, e.g., loyalty to the institution rather than to the juvenile. If trust is lacking, the physician will not have the juvenile's cooperation, and the juvenile may be reluctant to provide the physician with vital information. Therefore, there must be a strict separation of medical and legal issues within the institution. The institution's medical personnel should not be engaged in collecting evidence or participating in other judicial proceedings against the juvenile. Exceptions to this rule may exist if the juvenile personally asks medical personnel to perform a service the juvenile believes to be in his or her best interest. In most cases, judicial authorities should bring in outside medical personnel to collect evidence. Likewise, medical records should be safeguarded and released to nonmedical personnel only after a court subpoena is issued.

Confidentiality and Separation of Responsibilities

Careworkers who work within the medical area often become aware of confidential medical information. Having access to medical records and overhearing private conversations are two common modes of information transfer. In addition, some information may be explicitly revealed, such as a juvenile's positive HIV (human immunodeficiency virus) status. Medical ethics, state laws, and common decency demand that staff keep all medical information confidential, especially from juveniles. Juveniles acting as trustees within institutions must never be permitted to come into contact with confidential information, even if it is in sealed containers. If a careworker believes that information he or she has should be disseminated further he or she should first discuss it with the health care authority in charge of the medical unit.

Initial Health Status Screening

Immediately on arrival at a detention facility the juvenile should undergo a medical evaluation to determine that he or she is well enough for detention. The presence of communicable diseases, which could threaten the rest of the population, should be ruled out. The evaluation is usually done by a trained nurse using a standard form. Small institutions may elect for this evaluation to be done at a local hospital, in the emergency department, or at the outpatient clinic.

If juveniles arrive twenty-four hours a day, then health screening is necessary twenty-four hours a day. The screening includes gathering information

Medical ethics, state laws, and common decency demand that staff keep all medical information confidential, especially from juveniles.

in regard to demographic data, present illnesses, past medical history, current prescription drug use, and allergies. Information on past illicit drug and alcohol use should also be recorded. The assessment looks for current intoxication/overdose on drugs, as well as injuries that may have been sustained just before or while being taken into custody, e.g., injuries from auto accidents or canine bites. The juvenile's heart and respiratory rate, blood pressure, weight, height, and visual acuity are measured. Many institutions elect to draw a blood sample to test for syphilis and to test urine with a dipstick to help rule out infection or kidney problems. If medical staff are not available twenty-four hours a day, custody staff may be trained to conduct a limited medical assessment.

A complete physical exam may be conducted within a few days of the juvenile's arrival in detention. Local laws may mandate the length of time allowed before the exam must be completed. A focused medical history is taken to supplement the history already collected on arrival. The physician, nurse practitioner, or physician assistant completes a physical, paying special attention to the heart, lungs, skin, and musculoskeletal system. All sexually active females should have a pelvic examination because the rate of sexually transmissible disease is quite high in detained females. Males also require a careful exam of the penis, anus, and scrotum. At the end of the exam, immunizations and a test for tuberculosis can be administered.

Nursing Rounds

Each juvenile should have daily access to medical care providers in case a health problem has developed. In small institutions, juveniles may be brought to the nurse for evaluation and treatment. In larger settings, nurses make rounds in the living units several times a day to evaluate the sick and to dispense medication. Whatever the situation, the juvenile must be afforded privacy so that the other juveniles and staff do not eavesdrop on the juvenile's conversation with the nurse. Following nursing protocols, nurses may treat minor illness on the spot thus saving physician time and preventing complications that may result if treatment were delayed. Those juveniles who need a physician's evaluation can be referred to the next sick call. Careworkers must ensure juveniles have access to medical personnel during these rounds.

Clinic or Sick Call

Physician services must be available on a regular basis. Many large institutions have physicians on the premises for several hours each day, while smaller facilities may have a physician present for only a few hours each week. In the latter case, emergency care must be available from an emergency department twenty-four hours a day, and procedures must be in place so that there is no delay in getting care. The place where the physician sees juveniles must provide privacy, be adequately lit, and contain the furniture and equipment that is needed to provide diagnosis and treatment.

Dispensing Medication

Medication may be dispensed on the living units, in the clinic, or both. In any case, there must be security to prevent theft and privacy because some medications are easily recognizable. Dispensing liquid forms of psychiatric or abused drugs help ensure that the juvenile will actually ingest the medication. Careworkers and nursing staff must be alert and ensure that juveniles are swallowing their medicines and that they are not hording or selling them. Juveniles may attempt to save enough medication to commit suicide by drug overdose.

Infirmary Care

Not all institutions will elect to have an infirmary. Small facilities may house mildly ill juveniles in their regular living units, providing regular attendance by a nurse or physician during the day. In this situation, very ill juveniles must be moved to a hospital.

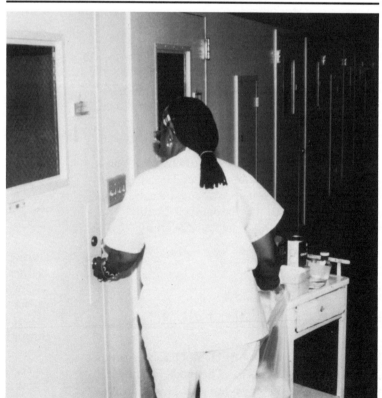

In some large institutions, nurses make rounds in the living units several times a day to evaluate the sick and to dispense medication.

Large institutions are more likely to have twenty-four-hour nursing coverage, which allows the operation of a formal infirmary. The severity of illnesses will range from mild (e.g., a condition that would keep a juvenile home from school) to serious (e.g., a condition that requires hospitalization). The decision to transfer a juvenile to a hospital depends on the degree of illness, the level of care available, and the potential for rapid change in the juvenile's condition. A physician makes this medical judgment.

Typical conditions seen in an infirmary include fevers, communicable infectious diseases, diagnostic problems resulting in disability, post-operative patients, serious infections requiring regular antibiotics, organ failures, and juveniles who cannot walk because of injuries or leg casts. Psychiatric patients are sometimes housed in the infirmary also. This practice allows the medical physician, as well as the psychiatric practitioner, to have daily contact with mentally ill juveniles. This daily contact is important because these juveniles might develop side effects from their medication or become sick with a medical illness. The infirmary can also be used to collect specimens, such as early morning blood, urine, or stool, that might otherwise be difficult to obtain.

Each infirmary room should contain a bed, desk, seat, and a toilet. The latter is needed because many patients have an urgent and immediate need to use a toilet. Some rooms may be equipped with a camera for monitoring potentially injurious juveniles.

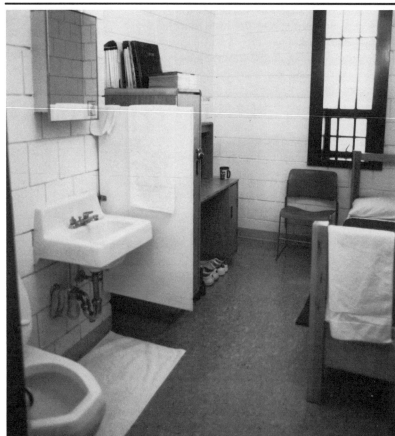

Each infirmary room should contain a bed, desk, seat, and a toilet.

Medical Services in Locked or Disciplinary Units

Juveniles held in seclusion may not be able to attend sick call. Arrangements must be made for these juveniles to be visited by a nurse or physician at least daily. If medical staff feel the juvenile should be brought to the infirmary or medical treatment area, the juvenile should be moved with appropriate restraints. Juveniles who repeatedly become confined to disciplinary units may be at high risk for self-destructive behavior. They should be considered for referral for mental health evaluation.

Cardiopulmonary Resuscitation

During cardiac arrest the heart stops and blood flow to the brain ceases, leading to brain death within five or six minutes. In juveniles and young adults, cardiac arrest is often the result of suicide attempts or diseases that interrupt the normal electrical flow through the heart causing cardiac dysrhythmia. These are very rare events, but careworkers who work with a large number of juveniles may eventually witness a cardiac arrest. Unfortunately, many juveniles who experience cardiac arrest never have warning symptoms or problems that allow intervention before the potentially fatal event.

Rescuers using cardiopulmonary resuscitation (CPR) can maintain blood flow to the brain until the heart can be restarted. CPR involves assisting the heart through chest compressions while adding oxygen to the blood by breathing directly into the victim's mouth to force air into the lungs. Regular training programs within institutions teach CPR to new staff and refresher courses to staff every few years. CPR must be learned by demonstration and practice and cannot be learned by reading a publication.

HIV and AIDS

Infection with human immunodeficiency virus (HIV) eventually leads to the development of acquired immune deficiency syndrome (AIDS), a fatal, incurable disease that affects the body's ability to fight off cancers and infections. At the time of initial infection (the primary infection) the person may become sick with a flu-like illness that lasts from several days to weeks. However, many do not become sick during the primary infection. The virus first attacks a specific blood cell called a helper T cell. During this first stage, the virus is produced in large numbers by the body, and the infected person is believed to be more capable of passing the infection on to others.

Once the primary infection phase passes, a quiet phase begins and may last several years. During this time, the person is well and may be unaware of the infection. The person still can pass on the infection, but at a lesser rate than during the primary infection phase. During this quiet phase, the number of helper T cells gradually falls until there are too few left to fight off diseases. At first the person develops minor infections, such as yeast infections in the mouth or a recurrence of chicken pox called herpes zoster. Laboratories can now measure the number of helper T cells, a process that provides a more accurate estimate of disease progression. The number of helper T cells fluctuates between 400 and 1500 in healthy individuals, with the usual number over 1000. When the number of helper T cells of an HIV-infected person declines to 500, most authorities suggest beginning use of the antiretroviral drug zidovudine (once called AZT now called ZVD), which slows the progression of the illness.

The actual diagnosis of AIDS is made when the individual develops a serious opportunistic infection, such as pneumocystis pneumonia, or when the number of helper T cells falls below 200. At the level of 200, additional drugs are used to help prevent the occurrence of opportunistic infections. Even with low levels of helper T cells the individual can remain well and productive if infections are avoided.

HIV can become resistant to ZVD, which means the drug no longer slows the rate of progression. Recently, several other drugs that can be used alone or in combination with ZVD have become available. These drugs work well for some individuals, but for others the disease continues to weaken the immune system. When the level of helper T cells is less than 50, the infected person is usually quite frail and requires significant medical care. However, a few individuals remain well even at these low levels. The rate of HIV progression varies from person to person, but the average interval from initial infection to a diagnosis of AIDS is currently believed to be ten years.

HIV Diagnosis

Because the disease is silent (asymptomatic) for years, alternative methods of diagnosis are necessary. A blood test that measures the human body's reaction to HIV can detect the infection in a person beginning about one-and-a-half to three months after the primary infection. A simple, quick

---

A blood test that measures the human body's reaction to HIV can detect the infection in a person beginning about one-and-a-half to three months after the primary infection.

---

screening test is done first, and if the result is positive, a more expensive and complicated test called a Western Blot is performed to confirm that the infection is present. Despite the double testing, all medical tests have some false results. When many individuals at low risk for HIV infection are tested, a few will inevitably receive a false positive result. Therefore, all positive tests should be repeated before concluding that a person is HIV positive. In some cases, additional tests, such as tests that measure the number of helper T cells, should also be performed to confirm that HIV is the cause of a positive test result.

How HIV Is Transmitted

Most cases of HIV occur in homosexual or bisexual men, intravenous drug users, or the sexual partners of these individuals. Additional cases are found in hemophiliacs and persons who received infected blood or blood products before testing for the virus began in 1985. HIV-positive mothers have about a 30 percent risk of infecting their babies. Women who become infected during their pregnancy or who have AIDS have a greater risk of passing the virus to their infants (Pizzo & Butler 1991; Van de Perre et al 1991).

As the virus spreads into the heterosexual population through intravenous drug users and their sex partners, more and more infections will result from heterosexual contacts. Juveniles have high rates of sexually transmissible diseases and are therefore at risk for contracting the virus.

Transmission cannot take place through casual contact, such as shaking hands, sharing toilets, or sharing living spaces. Skin offers protection from penetration of viruses and bacteria. HIV is found primarily in blood and sexual fluids. Although it has been detected in very small quantities in other fluids, the virus in these fluids appears to be incapable of causing infection. The virus is difficult to transmit, and special conditions are required for transmission to take place.

There must be blood-to-blood contact as happens in sharing needles during intravenous drug use. Or sexual fluids must contact blood as happens in some sexual practices, such as anal intercourse or, to a lesser degree, vaginal intercourse. During vaginal intercourse, male to female transmission occurs more frequently than female to male.

Transmission does not happen

- during casual contact with infected individuals

- through the air

- through contact with nonliving objects, i.e., books or eating utensils

- by mosquito bites or other insect contacts

- among health care personnel and patients, even when contact is prolonged. Even under extreme circumstances, such as an HIV-contaminated needle stick, the risk of transmission is only 1 chance in 260 (Marcus & CDC Cooperative Needlestick Group 1988). Splashes of contaminated blood hitting the eye or large open wounds have rarely resulted in transmission.

- from deep kissing, human bites, or contact externally with body fluids, such as spitting or urinating on to intact skin

Objects, such as razors, that may have blood on them should not be shared because of the risk of transmitting many diseases, including HIV.

Prevention of Infection

Those at risk for infection are individuals who engage in unsafe sexual practices, especially with persons belonging to high-risk groups, i.e., homosexuals, bisexuals, or intravenous drug users. Preventing these risk behaviors will reasonably control the transmission of the virus. Although careworkers do not engage in any of these behaviors with juveniles, they need to minimize exposure to bodily fluids through accidents or fights (even though such exposures is unlikely to result in transmission). Because most individuals with HIV are asymptomatic and thus not identifiable, all blood spills should be considered infectious, not only for HIV but also for other diseases. Use of gloves and proper disinfection with any standard cleaner will adequately protect staff and juveniles.

The most useful way to prevent HIV infection in institutions is education of all staff and juveniles,

---

The most useful way to prevent HIV infection in institutions is education of all staff and juveniles, not only the high-risk persons.

---

not only the high-risk persons. Discussions of the cause and prevention of transmission, including using safe sex practices, limiting the number of partners, and avoiding contaminated needles and paraphernalia during intravenous drug use, must be repeated many times. To allay unfounded fears, staff and juveniles should also be educated about what does not lead to transmission. Institutional regulations prohibit sexual relations and unsupervised drug use, so normal supervision and security practices will curtail unsafe practices.

Detection of HIV-positive Juveniles

Diagnosing HIV-positive juveniles is important so treatment can begin early in the disease process when it will be most beneficial. Laws regarding testing of juveniles vary by location, but most states allow juveniles to consent to HIV testing. The lynch pin of successful HIV detection is trust of the medical and detention staff by juveniles. Juveniles are more likely to agree to voluntary testing if they feel secure and do not fear unwarranted reprisals or discrimination if they test positive.

Appropriate pre- and post-test counseling must accompany any HIV testing program. If local regulations require disclosure of a juvenile's HIV-positive status to nonmedical personnel, the juvenile should be so informed before testing. Staff who may need to be informed should be fully educated about confidentiality and the penalties under the law for breach of confidentiality. Other institutional regulations regarding HIV-infected juveniles must also be disclosed. Even when unfavorable events will happen if the juvenile tests positive, most juveniles will consent to testing if they understand the reasons and benefits of knowing their HIV status.

Some institutions have elected to isolate all their HIV-positive juveniles in one location, but most have not. It may be useful to place a newly diagnosed juvenile in the infirmary for a short time until the juvenile's initial reaction to having tested positive for the infection can be managed. Infirmary care allows daily contact with medical staff so questions can be answered and maximum support provided. Once the juvenile and staff feel he or she is ready, the juvenile can return to a regular living unit. If the juvenile's behavior is erratic or dangerous to others, then continuing infirmary care or other reasonable isolation may be necessary.

All those interacting with HIV-positive juveniles should strive to be supportive, understanding, reassuring, and responsive. Special counseling programs and individual treatment often help to prevent needless suffering and thus prevent undesirable behavioral reactions.

Epilepsy

The brain is a collection of nerve cells, all of which operate using very mild, controlled electrical current. Epilepsy results from uncontrolled electrical waves that begin in one area of the brain and spread to adjacent areas. Anyone may have a seizure under

---

All those interacting with HIV-positive juveniles should strive to be supportive, understanding, reassuring, and responsive.

---

extreme circumstances, but epileptics have a lower threshold than other persons and will seize more easily. Seizures (spells) can be provoked by fevers, illness, sleep deprivation, or in some cases, upsetting events.

During an epileptic spell, the juvenile may exhibit any of the following symptoms: seizures, sometimes referred to as fits or spells (convulsions), impairment of motor control (falling), loss of consciousness, and psychological or behavioral difficulties. Seizures are divided into three main types: grand mal, petit mal, and psychomotor episodes.

Grand mal seizures are often marked by loss of consciousness and violent movements. The juvenile loses consciousness and becomes stiff and barely breathes. Severe muscle twitching and shaking of the body follows. Breathing can be temporarily restricted, and the juvenile may turn blue for a few minutes. There can also be frothing at the mouth. Sometimes the bowels or the bladder are emptied during the course of an attack. The eyes may stare straight ahead, roll upward, or look to the right or left. Medical personnel who arrive after a seizure has ended may need to know which of the events happened during the seizure. This information can be useful in diagnosis, especially if this is the juvenile's first seizure.

Many epileptics experience a warning feeling (called an aura), which allows them to protect themselves before the attack begins by lying down;

but some do not, and they will fall down at the beginning of an attack. Some epileptics involuntarily emit a cry before their attack begins. Grand mal seizures are usually followed by a period of confusion and lethargy.

A petit mal seizure is marked by brief losses of consciousness lasting from a few seconds to half a minute. The juvenile does not loose muscle strength and therefore does not fall down. A juvenile experiencing a petit mal seizure may appear to be daydreaming or not paying attention. The juvenile is unconscious and unaware of what is going on around him or her during the time the seizure is happening. After the seizure, the juvenile returns to his or her normal state and is unaware the seizure happened. A juvenile can become injured during these seizures because of inattention.

During the psychomotor seizure, the epileptic has no convulsions but experiences reduced consciousness and loss of memory. The juvenile retains the ability to act, but in a purposeless fashion, often talking nonsense, making chewing movements with his or her mouth, and engaging in bizarre or occasionally threatening behavior. The psychomotor seizure is much less common than the grand and petit mal types.

Response to a Seizure

Emergency treatment of an epileptic convulsion involves realizing that it must run its course; there is nothing one can do to stop it. Because the seizure is often dramatic, both staff and juveniles may react inappropriately to the epileptic during and after the seizure. Staff must remain calm to prevent overreaction and to give others appropriate information after the seizure terminates. During a major attack, the epileptic will thrash about violently. A pillow or a substitute, such as a coat, may be placed under the juvenile's head to prevent bruising the face and scalp. Nearby objects on which the juvenile may be injured should be removed. If the juvenile appears to be choking, the tongue may have fallen into the back of the mouth, obstructing the airway. Simply rolling the epileptic onto his or her side allows the tongue to drop forward, out of the airway. Nothing should ever be forced into the mouth of an epileptic during a seizure. Putting an object or fingers into the mouth may result in broken teeth or bitten fingers. If the juvenile vomits, wipe the vomit out of the cheeks and keep the juvenile on his or her side to drain the vomit. Tight clothing, such as a belt or a closely fitting collar, should be loosened. After the thrashing stops, let the juvenile rest or sleep.

Treatment

Long-term medical control of epilepsy involves antiseizure medications. Once these drugs are prescribed, it is important for the juvenile to take them because sudden discontinuation of antiseizure drugs can cause severe, long-lasting convulsions. In fact, many seizures in previously controlled epileptics are the result of failure to take the prescribed medication. Some epilepsy-controlling medications may represent a temptation to other juveniles. Also, some epileptics resist taking their medication because of side effects, such as drowsiness. For these reasons, dispensing medication should be closely supervised, ideally by a trained medical staff member. Educating juveniles about the reasons for their medication and the transient nature of drug side effects will help compliance.

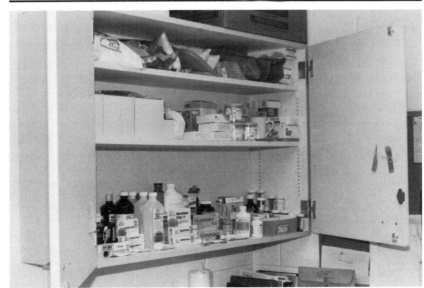

Dispensing medication should be closely supervised, ideally by a trained medical staff member.

Diabetes

The human body produces certain chemicals that enable it to use foods that are ingested. Insulin produced by the pancreas is a chemical that helps the body use sugars properly.

A diabetic produces too little or no insulin. When there is an imbalance between insulin and sugar, the body cannot use sugar as a fuel, and the person becomes ill. There are basically two types of diabetics. Most juvenile diabetics have type I and make no insulin. These individuals require insulin replacement by injection two or more times a day. The amount of sugar in the blood is usually measured three or four times every day to determine how much insulin is needed.

Adult diabetics usually have type II diabetes and make some but not enough insulin to meet all their needs. Diabetes in these individuals can be managed with a drug that increases the pancrea's supply of insulin. If the individual is overweight, then weight loss will decrease the amount of sugar the individual must process.

In both types of diabetes, careful attention must be paid to maintaining a diet that balances the proper proportions of sugar, protein, and fat. With proper attention, healthy diabetics can live and work in the same way as the nondiabetic.

Adolescence is a difficult time for diabetics because of the restrictions they must endure. Self-image suffers because the juvenile must face the life-long implications of a chronic illness. This can lead to oppositional behavior, including refusal to take insulin or cheating on the diet. Almost all juveniles do this occasionally but delinquent juveniles are more likely to continuously threaten noncompliance. Careworkers should be patient during these times—they should avoid threatening or blaming the juvenile.

The diabetic should be allowed to express his or her concerns regarding the disease and its treatment. After learning what the juvenile thinks and believes, the careworker or counselor can effectively guide the juvenile toward voluntary compliance. Occasionally, a psychiatric referral is needed when the diabetic is very depressed and may be using opposition to control others or to commit suicide.

Diabetes-related Problems

A diabetic coma involves a very high blood sugar and dehydration. This condition is usually the result of insulin withdrawal or infection and is sometimes aggravated by improper diet. If a diabetic coma is suspected, immediate medical attention is mandatory; without treatment, a diabetic coma can result in death or permanent, serious brain injury.

An insulin reaction (insulin shock) appears rapidly and is much more common than a diabetic coma. An insulin reaction occurs when there is too much insulin in the body.

Fortunately, most diabetics are familiar with their condition and are concerned about managing their lives in a way that will not aggravate the condition. In addition, most diabetic-related reactions are mild.

The diabetic should be allowed to express his or her concerns regarding the disease and its treatment.

Every diabetic who takes insulin should have some form of sugar available at all times to take in the event of an insulin reaction. In juvenile facilities this source of sugar may be kept in the living unit and classroom. A diabetic requesting sugar because of a reaction should always be given immediate access to juice or candy.

When an adverse insulin reaction comes on too fast for the diabetic to be capable of self-help, sugar in some form should be given immediately if the juvenile is still conscious. Insulin reactions can cause the diabetic to act silly or strange; staff dealing with diabetics should recognize unusual behavior as a possible insulin reaction and provide sugar. If the condition is not corrected promptly, the diabetic may loose consciousness entirely. If a diabetic becomes unconscious for any reason, medical assistance should be requested immediately. A coma can be fatal to a diabetic if medical attention is not received immediately. A diabetic's dose of daily insulin may vary over time and a physician is required to adjust the dose in response to the diabetic's previous blood sugar levels.

As a part of the diabetic's regular medical treatment program, food intake should be kept constant from day to day. Some diabetics may receive a "fifth feeding" in the form of a bedtime snack to keep their food intake constant throughout the day.

Tuberculosis

Tuberculosis (TB) was once thought to be in decline and under control in the United States. However, over the past decade the number of cases of active TB has increased, especially in the detained adult population and among individuals with HIV. Institutions dealing with detained juveniles must screen all their new arrivals with a skin test to detect TB. Prompt identification of juveniles with active (contagious) or inactive (noncontagious) TB allows appropriate treatment and the prevention of potential epidemics within the institution. Most institutions require staff to be tested for TB before beginning employment and may periodically screen employees.

Sexually Transmissible Diseases

Teenagers, and especially risk-taking teenagers, frequently engage in sexual activities and as a consequence have high rates of sexually transmissible diseases. In major cities the rates of sexually transmissible disease are high. In Los Angeles County, 15 percent of males and 45 percent of females entering detention will have at least one sexually transmissible disease. Most of these infections can be detected by testing the urine of males and doing a pelvic examination of females.

Common Infections

The adolescent years may involve a high rate of infectious diseases, many of which require isolation of the juvenile until the infection is treated or naturally resolves. Juveniles suffering from chicken pox, herpes zoster (a recurrence of chicken pox), or impetigo will usually need to be isolated.

Sports Injuries

The daily sports activities of juveniles cause a variety of injuries to bones, muscles, and organs. Level playing fields, careful supervision, and

appropriate exclusion of injured juveniles can reduce the number of serious injuries suffered during recreation periods. Juveniles who become injured should be evaluated by a physician before they are permitted to resume play.

Asthma and Other Chronic Diseases

Juveniles with known chronic illnesses present a management dilemma to medical staff, as well as other personnel. In addition to providing for the medical needs of these juveniles, staff must occasionally deal with juveniles who may exaggerate their difficulties or fake new symptoms for nonmedical reasons, special privileges, individual attention, or excuses from physical activity. In a few instances, a juvenile may wish to cause disruption.

On the other hand, juveniles with legitimate chronic illnesses are also likely to experience significant symptoms, which may result from complications of the basic illness or even the development of new diseases. Telling the difference between real and faked or exaggerated complaints can be difficult, even for a physician. Although some judgment must be exercised, the careworker should always make a medical referral if there is any reasonable doubt about the juvenile's need to receive medical care. Even a known malingerer may develop a real disease. Careworkers must avoid premature judgments influenced by a juvenile's previous deceptive behavior.

Individuals who suffer from asthma are subject to sudden periodic episodes during which the small air passages (bronchial tubes) inside their lungs become narrowed, causing a failure to inhale and exhale enough air. This causes a decrease in oxygen getting into the body. Some incidents are mild and the individual responds readily to inhaled medication. Inhalers should be kept under the control of medical personnel or, during off periods, under the control of corrections staff. Occasionally, inhalers do not work, and more serious airway obstruction may occur. An asthmatic appearing to have difficulty breathing should be referred to immediate medical care.

Juveniles are also subject to hyperventilation spells, which can be confused with asthma. During an attack, the juvenile first experiences the sensation of a tight chest and inability to catch his or her breath. This results in very rapid breathing, which

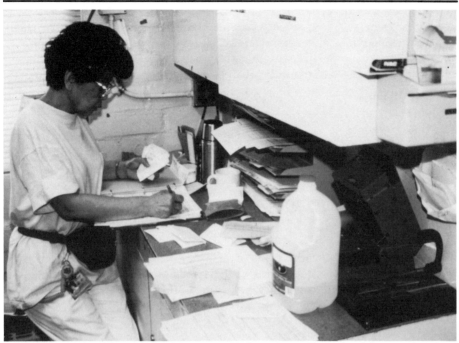
Careworkers should notify health care staff about juveniles' complaints so that they may be documented and evaluated.

may misunderstand court proceedings, placement orders, or other judicial events. They may wish to be with a friend and try to manipulate a move to join the friend. Malingering may also be misdiagnosed for some juveniles suffering psychosomatic illness brought on by stress. Many juveniles experience significant stress from school failure, parental neglect, violent surroundings, and loss of family members and friends. Although these juveniles may not be suffering from a documentable physical illness, they are suffering from real pain and discomfort.

Chronic complaining may also be a symptom of depression or an impending suicide attempt. Despite its unpleasant nature, chronic complaining should be taken seriously as a symptom deserving further evaluation.

in turn causes tingling in the hands and feet and light-headedness. These unpleasant sensations cause the juvenile to panic and breath faster. Most spells stop after a few minutes, but occasionally the juvenile may lose consciousness, at which time the breathing returns to normal, and he or she regains consciousness. These attacks can be triggered by stress or a fearful event or memory, or the attacks can come on spontaneously, without an identifiable cause. Once a hyperventilation spell is recognized, it can be managed by having the juvenile breathe into a paper bag. This prevents the excess escape of carbon dioxide and stops the unpleasant side effects of too rapid breathing.

Malingering and Chronic Complaining

Juveniles who pretend to be ill to arouse sympathy or to manipulate are defined as malingering. Detained juveniles rarely malinger, and when they do there is often a reason for the behavior. Careful, sympathetic interviewing of malingering juveniles usually reveals the reason for the malingering. Juveniles may malinger because they are afraid of bodily injury from others on the living unit. They

Hidden Medical Problems

Occasionally a juvenile may have a physical problem that manifests itself through behavior abnormalities. Hearing problems caused by holes in the eardrum or other damage to the ear may result in loud talking or failure to follow verbal directions. Poor vision can lead to failure to follow visual directions or poor school performance. Attention deficit disorder and hyperactivity manifests itself in an inability to sit still and to keep to one task for longer than a few minutes. Petit mal epilepsy appears as daydreaming or failure to pay attention. Enuresis, bed wetting, may be caused by bladder infections or may run in families. Stool withholding and the resulting incontinence of bowel movements (encopresis) may be due to severe stress or sexual abuse. Poor coordination can be caused by birth trauma that affected portions of the brain. This particular deficit may not be treatable, but once understood the juvenile can be better counseled as to what he or she can expect to accomplish. There are also some genetic disorders, such a Klinefelter's syndrome, which result in behavioral problems.

Many of these problems are detectable during a complete physical examination. Although all these problems are individually quite rare, when added together the sum is quite large. Careworkers who encounter a juvenile who seems different or unusual should refer the juvenile for a medical evaluation.

Dental Care

Many juveniles enter detention with dental needs. There are many reasons for this, including lack of money, lack of parental supervision, and poor understanding of the importance of regular dental care. Fear also plays a powerful role in causing some individuals to defer dental care. The controlled time of detention can be used to teach juveniles the importance of proper dental care. Careworkers should listen to the juvenile's concerns and provide guidance and information based on these concerns. Careworkers should not joke about the dental procedure or tease the juvenile about his or her concerns; this will create undue anxieties and make it difficult to allay irrational fears.

Juveniles may have many dental problems, including gum disease and dental decay, from poor flossing and brushing. These problems, although threatening to the integrity of the tooth, may not be painful, and the juvenile may wish to ignore them. Eventually small problems will progress to large cavities or dental abbesses, which are painful and require emergency dental care. For some dental problems, such as an abscess, a physician can prescribe antibiotics to relieve pain until the dentist can provide definitive care.

Impacted wisdom teeth commonly affect juveniles between the ages of 16 and 20. The juvenile may have pain in the back of the jaw, pain with chewing, loose flaps of skin that trap food, or less common, a headache or earache. Because impacted teeth are so common, large institutions often have an oral surgeon on staff to deal with them. Oral surgeons can also stabilize broken jaws, suture facial lacerations, and remove growths from the mouth. The number of trips to an oral surgeon outside the institution can be substantially reduced by having

---

The controlled time of detention can be used to teach juveniles the importance of proper dental care.

---

the services of an oral surgeon on site. An additional advantage of an in-house oral surgeon is his or her familiarity with the juveniles. Outside practitioners may lack the patience and empathy needed to work successfully with this special population.

Summary

It is important for careworkers to be alert and responsive to juveniles' health care needs. Careworkers must maintain a high level of professionalism when dealing with the issues of confidentiality and the juveniles' right to privacy. When a careworker expresses concern and compassion, the juvenile who needs medical attention is more likely to ask for it and to follow instructions from medical personnel.

Although careworkers are not qualified to treat juveniles for medical problems, they are a vital link between juveniles and access to medical services. Referral to medical staff and documentation of a juvenile's symptoms and behavior by a careworker help trained medical staff diagnose and treat the juvenile.

APPLICABLE ACA STANDARDS
3-JTS-5A–5B
3-JDF-5A

11

Food Service for Juveniles

By Deborah Martinez and Alice Sanchez, R.D.

Food service is an important part of institutional life. A comprehensive food service program must be developed if a facility is to meet the unique needs of its juvenile population.

The role of the food service program in today's juvenile correctional environment has taken on new significance. Juvenile health, nutrition, and morale in this environment are all directly related to the effectiveness of the food service program. The mission of providing juvenile offenders with three meals a day, for 365 days a year, without fail, becomes more of a challenge when the meals served must be tailored to appeal to a particular age group whose tastes and eating habits are not fully matured.

Meals served to incarcerated juveniles must be nutritionally balanced and calorically adequate. They must be tasty, appealing, and served in an aesthetically acceptable manner to avoid conduct and behavior problems. If juveniles believe the facility's staff and management have maximized their efforts to provide a safe and appealing program, conduct could improve.

Menu Planning and Development

The menu is one of the most important aspects in the food service program. Meals must be planned to meet the juveniles' nutritional and caloric

---

Juvenile health, nutrition, and morale are directly related to the effectiveness of the food service program.

---

requirements, as well as to provide popular and appealing selections they will eat. The goal should be to plan each meal to include menu items that are acceptable to juveniles so that they will want to consume the full meal. Only then will juveniles receive the full nutritional value of the meals.

Juvenile Nutrition

Juveniles typically have less than desirable eating habits. Nutritional guidelines for juveniles are extrapolations from the recommendations for

Deborah Martinez is a food service director for Sun West Services, a food management company, at the New Mexico Youth Diagnostic and Development Center at Albuquerque, New Mexico.

Alice Sanchez, R.D., is a regional dietitian and food service director for Sun West Services and works in the company's Arizona unit serving the Sanders Unified School District.

children and adults. Recommended dietary allowances relate to the general time and rate of the juvenile's growth spurt. The amount of food needed by any given juvenile depends on the individual, but meals must be planned according to an established daily food choices pattern (Table 8-1). This pattern is designed to maintain and achieve optimal nutritional status while recognizing that juveniles have different food preferences.

A pleasant dining room atmosphere enhances the attractiveness of the meal served.

If a facility is participating in the National School Breakfast Program and the National School Lunch Program, breakfast and lunch meals should be planned in accordance with U.S. Department of Agriculture (USDA) guidelines. Meal patterns provide nutritionally balanced meals with food items selected from the various food component groups. By offering choices of different foods from each component food group, the juvenile has the opportunity to make selections.

Table 8-1. Daily Food Choices Pattern

Food Group	Suggested Daily Servings
Breads, cereal, and other grain products (includes several servings a day of whole-grain products)	6 to 11
Fruit	2 to 4
Vegetables (includes all types, with dark green leafy vegetables and dry beans and peas used several times per week)	3 to 5
Meat, poultry, fish, and alternatives (5 to 7 ounces, lean, per serving)	2 to 3
Milk, cheese, yogurt, etc.	4
Fats and sweets	Keep to a minimum

Menu Cycles and Cost Effectiveness

Menus should be planned in six-week cycles. Planning in this way helps to make production estimates more accurate, minimize food waste, and keep food costs down. The proper mix, frequency, and selection of menu items appropriate for this special age group are important elements in making menus appealing and effective. In addition, menus should reflect the population's cultural and ethnic preferences as much as possible. The menu cycle is designed to correspond with seasonal variations. Changing the menu occasionally to take advantage of seasonal "good buys" will lower food costs and add variety to the menu at the same time.

USDA surplus food commodities are available for facilities operating under the National School Lunch Program. Proper handling and usage procedures must be followed to qualify for continued receipt of these products. By incorporating these commodities into the menu, cost containment becomes much easier. The menu should be reviewed annually, if not quarterly, to evaluate menu acceptability and cost effectiveness.

Snacks, Special Diets, and Special Events

To meet caloric requirements for juveniles, between-meal snacks or meal supplements should be provided in the mid-afternoon or evening. These snacks should be planned in accordance with the daily food choices pattern and also with the six-week cycle. Additional meal supplements may be provided to juveniles requiring higher caloric needs.

Most facilities allow substitutions of the regular menu on a case-by-case basis if a juvenile is unable to consume the regular menu items because of medical or other special dietary needs (i.e., lactose intolerance, allergy, specific caloric needs for weight gain and/or weight reduction, chewing problems, or other handicaps that restrict the diet). All exceptions must be supported by a statement from a medical authority that includes recommended substitute foods. These statements should be kept on file. In addition to medical and dietary exceptions, variations in the menu are allowed for juveniles to meet religious or ethnic special needs. Such variations must be nutritionally sound and should be supported by an authentic religious or ethnic authority.

A program of special theme and holiday meals should be incorporated into menu planning to increase juvenile morale and to avoid menu boredom. Traditional holidays, local celebrations, and heritage recognition can form the basis of this program.

Maintaining Program Efficiency

An effective and efficient food service program gives attention to each of the fundamental elements of a food service operation: purchasing and inventory control, food production, personnel management, tool control measures, and personal hygiene. The health and well-being of every juvenile and staff member depend on these practices being professionally maintained. Written policies, practices, controls, and systems should always be in place to ensure compliance.

Purchasing, Receiving, Storage, and Inventory Practices

Purchasing efficiently is based on an exact standard of quality and competitive bidding. Monthly bids are obtained for most food items following a detailed set of USDA, state, and local guidelines to ensure that the purchasing system functions properly. Food specifications are defined to fit a facility's needs in light of menu, quality and

quantity needed, availability, and storage capacity available. Orders for most food products and supplies are placed weekly; some perishable goods must be obtained more frequently (e.g., fresh fruits and vegetables, bakery goods, and dairy products).

The inspection of foods by receiving personnel is an important part of cost and quality control. The receiving employee is trained to accept only top-grade supplies. All food items received are counted, verified, and weighed in the receiving area. Unacceptable products are rejected, and a notation is made on the delivery receipt and order form.

Food products are stored where appropriate: dry storage, refrigerator, or freezer. A written record of the temperatures in each unit is maintained and posted at all times. Proper temperatures for storage are as follows:

1. Dry goods should be stored at 60 to 68 degrees Fahrenheit.

2. Meats should be stored at 34 to 38 degrees Fahrenheit, otherwise they should be frozen.

3. Dairy products should be stored at 34 to 38 degrees Fahrenheit.

4. Frozen foods should be stored at -10 to -20 degrees Fahrenheit.

5. Produce should be stored at 36 to 40 degrees Fahrenheit.

Case goods are stored in such a manner that the oldest cases are used first (first in, first out). Cases are dated at the time they are placed in storage, and all items are stored off the floor on pallets or shelving. The storeroom is arranged in an order that allows food to be inventoried by similar groups. Storage areas should be dry and well-ventilated. Accurate food management is obtained by monthly inventories. The food cost for each month is calculated from the inventory and purchasing records. The total value of the inventory is closely examined each month to make sure that it is not significantly increasing. Large inventories can result in a deterioration of food quality, can invite pilferage, and can detract from available cash reserves. Foods that have been in storage for a long period of time may be used through menu changes.

Food Production Operations

To ensure proper food production planning a food production record should be maintained daily. This record indicates the standardized recipe to be used and instructions on handling leftovers, should they exist. It includes the menus for breakfast, lunch, dinner, and snacks. The completed production record serves as the primary source of information about the food control system in the kitchen.

Standardized recipes are used to prepare all food items in which more than one ingredient is used. This practice ensures a uniform, high-quality product and maintains control over cost. Standard portion control is important for any food service facility. It ensures compliance with required meal patterns and dietary guidelines and aids in controlling food production costs. Each food item is assigned the exact weight, size, or count of the portion size. The portion size is listed on the standard recipe and production sheet. Portion sizes can be best controlled through effective training and close supervision.

Civilian Kitchen Personnel

Food service personnel in a juvenile institution have a dual role. They are expected to perform their culinary tasks in an expert manner, as well as follow recipes and other professional food production procedures. They act as role models for the juveniles. They have a unique opportunity to teach personal hygiene, proper dining room behavior, and healthy food selections. Staff members should always be in a "training mode," receiving updated information on new production methods and new control procedures. The success and positive attitude of the civilian staff is a cornerstone of the success of the entire food service program.

Tool Control Measures

Tool control in a juvenile food service operation is concerned primarily with knives and other sharp items ("sharps"). In most facilities, kitchen tools are stored in a locked box or cabinet located in a secure area. A cabinet with a safety glass front is most efficient because it allows quick visual checks without much effort. Inside the cabinet, each tool is hung from hooks and outlined with a permanent marker so that missing tools are easily identified. When a staff member needs to use a tool, a durable metal tag with that person's identifier is placed on the hook to make clear who has the item. A written

inventory of all items in the knife cabinet must be kept and be easily accessible. At each shift change a designated staff person should verify the location of all sharps and initial the inventory list. This knife control inventory should also be checked no less than monthly by correctional staff on a regular basis.

Sanitation and Personal Hygiene

Each juvenile food service operation must maintain high sanitation standards. An inspection checklist should be used to conduct safety and sanitation inspections and to enforce compliance with established standards.

A systematic pest control program should be constantly maintained in the facility. Cleaning schedules should be planned in writing and posted in a conspicuous place. Cleaning products and tools should be available to efficiently perform any and all cleaning tasks. Procedures for proper handling

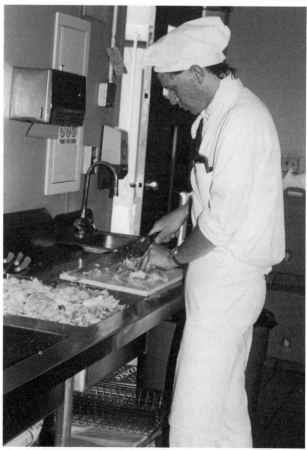

Food service personnel are expected to perform their culinary tasks in an expert manner.

and removal of trash and grease should be developed, written, and posted.

The personal hygiene policy for the facility should clearly describe the standards of cleanliness expected of each employee and juvenile food service worker. Personal cleanliness and personal habits should be closely observed. Unacceptable work habits and unsanitary practices should be immediately identified by the supervisor.

Employees who report to work ill (i.e., elevated temperature, severe coughing, sneezing) should not be allowed to remain. Employees exposed to contagious diseases must first be cleared by the facility's medical authority before returning to work. Skin infections and/or irritations must always be covered for an employee to work in a designated food area.

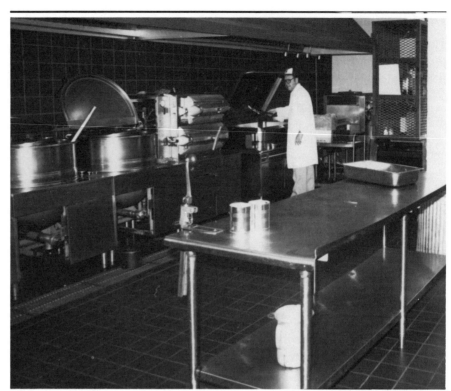
Each juvenile food service operation must maintain high sanitation standards.

Food Service and the Juvenile Population

Meal Service Considerations

Gathering large numbers of juveniles together in a confined space, such as a dining room, creates the potential for problems. Serious disturbances and security risks can be limited if an orderly system of food serving lines and juvenile seating arrangements is enforced. The scheduled meal time should require appropriate dress and personal cleanliness for each juvenile, and serving schedules should allow reasonable time for juveniles to finish their meals. Some meal schedules are determined by housing arrangements or units.

Careworkers should work with the facility's food service manager and administration to determine the most effective path for receiving meals and to limit unnecessary movement by juveniles. A

cafeteria-style steam table serving line should be located close to the kitchen. This arrangement allows ease of food movement, maintenance of food temperatures, and supervisory space for careworkers to observe and monitor juvenile activities while at the serving line.

It is the joint responsibility of the careworkers and the food service staff to monitor and correct any serving problems. Juvenile food service workers have a tendency to serve their friends larger portions than is customary, and this overportioning could erupt into disputes over favoritism. Close staff supervision can deter this practice and prevent it from becoming a major problem.

Each institution should evaluate its particular security and safety needs based on its population and dining room architecture. Although it is necessary to maintain security at all times, a pleasant dining room atmosphere will enhance the attractiveness of the meal served and will help juveniles to think of meal time as a pleasurable experience. The food service staff's pride in providing a healthful, attractive meal in a pleasant atmosphere will have a positive affect on the juveniles and will boost morale.

Juvenile Involvement in Food Services

Training juveniles to work in a food service operation is a challenging and time-consuming undertaking. A program built on juvenile incentives and some deterrents makes the task much easier. Incentives may include the opportunity to earn a food service certificate or letter of recognition that juveniles can take with them when they leave the institution, incentive pay, special snacks, and other privileges, such as watching a movie. Incentives can motivate juveniles to work in food service and increase the program's pool of juvenile kitchen workers. Just as a hierarchy of incentives helps to motivate the juveniles, a hierarchy of deterrents helps to discipline the juveniles when necessary. Deterrents may include written warnings, suspension of kitchen duties, or other negative penalties. If the institution creates a program where it is a privilege to work in food services, more juveniles will want to participate in the program.

A structured level system should be used when training juveniles. The level system promotes the juvenile worker from simple to more difficult food service tasks (i.e., pots and pans duty to dish machine duty to line serving duty). Juveniles often have short memories and cannot remember a long list of verbal assignments recited in one quick breath. Job descriptions for each juvenile food service worker position should be developed and posted for reference.

Close supervision of juvenile food service workers is mandatory. Many detained juveniles have never washed a pan or peeled a potato. They need constant encouragement and direction. Positive training steadily builds a juvenile's confidence and morale. Close supervision also means limiting juvenile access to the major food production to prevent opportunities a juvenile might have to contaminate food products.

Juvenile Feedback on Food Services

Allowing juvenile representatives the opportunity to participate in evaluating and planning food service programs stimulates interest in the food service operation and builds positive morale. Quarterly meetings with representatives from each housing unit to discuss elements of the program can limit the number of complaints and outbursts in the dining room by educating juveniles on the complexities of providing food service. Participating in menu planning and in improving the dining atmosphere helps juveniles feel they are a part of the solution and are contributing to an improvement. Decisions made by corrections administration with the participation of juvenile representatives will rarely be criticized.

Juvenile involvement in planning morale boosters for both the juvenile population and careworkers can produce positive results. Special meals with decorations, dances, and barbecues can

---

Positive training steadily builds a juvenile's confidence and morale.

---

be implemented to add variety to the dining ritual. Juveniles can be placed in charge of decorations, or poster contests may be organized to stimulate teamwork.

ACA Standards and Application

American Correctional Association standards for food services operations clearly define all aspects of kitchen operations that must be monitored. The standards address services, programs, and operations essential to good correctional management, including staff training and development, physical plant, safety, sanitation, rules, and discipline. Being accredited by ACA signifies that the facility has passed a strict audit of all departmental facets.

Some specific requirements are as follows:

1. The food service manager inspects all areas and equipment related to food preparation regularly.

2. Food service workers must be in good health and free from communicable diseases and open or infected sores.

3. All persons involved in preparing food must be cleared by the medical authority prior to and periodically checked during their employ.

Summary

The food service program within a juvenile corrections facility is an integral component of the juvenile facility's operation. By consistently serving nutritious and tasteful meals in a sanitary environment, the health and conduct of the juvenile is ensured. Because of the magnified nature of food service, a less than adequate program could impair the effectiveness of other institutional programs or offerings, not to mention be the cause of a serious disturbance.

The success of the food service program and its effect on the juveniles is a collaborative effort between food service staff and management and the corrections administration and careworkers. Security and supervision of the juveniles, fair food distribution, and orderly conduct in the dining areas must be regulated for the meals, themselves, to be effective.

APPLICABLE ACA STANDARDS

3-JTS-4A-01–15
3-JDF-4A-01–14

12

Care of the Physical Plant

By Warren H. Albrecht

Some careworkers may think the care of the physical plant is someone else's responsibility. This is not true. The condition of the physical plant reflects the careworkers' personal standards, care, and concern for juveniles.

The kind of environment established through continuous care of a physical plant begins with pride of ownership by all staff, but particularly careworkers and other line staff, such as juvenile officers, youth aides, and others. The persons in those positions are responsible for the direct supervision, care, and custody of juveniles placed in juvenile facilities.

The condition of the physical plant reflects the careworkers' personal standards, care, and concern for juveniles.

Because careworkers have the most contact with the juveniles in their care, they have the greatest opportunity to shape values through actively modeling behavior. Taking and sharing pride in

Warren H. Albrecht is director of the MacCormick Secure Center, New York State Division of Youth, in Brooktondale, New York.

sanitation and housekeeping practices is important to a juvenile's sense of achievement and self-esteem. The skills and work philosophy learned in the upkeep of the facility will benefit the juveniles at home and at work. The care of physical plant is everyone's job.

Everyday Routines

In *Standards for Juvenile Training Schools*, third edition, Standard 3-JTS-4B-06 states: "There is a written housekeeping plan for the facility's physical plant." Because the term "facility" may mean a campus with cottages and program support buildings or an institution under one roof, multi-story or mega-building, the housekeeping plan could vary in terms of staff and juvenile responsibility. There are, however, some practices that need to be part of everyday routine, regardless of facility dimensions:

1. Each juvenile in a living unit should be assigned a cleaning chore to be completed daily prior to breakfast.

2. Unit chore assignments should be rotated weekly by staff and posted at the start of each week.

3. Each juvenile must be held accountable for maintaining his or her room and/or area in a sanitary, neat, and orderly fashion. It may be helpful to limit the amount and kinds of items for which a juvenile is responsible by establishing a room or dorm articles list.

4. Prior to breakfast, unit and/or central service staff should conduct an inspection of the living unit and document the overall cleanliness.

5. If a juvenile's work is considered unsatisfactory, staff should instruct the juvenile to redo the task. Ratings may be recorded for the juvenile's second effort to complete the assignment. Noncompliance should be dealt with in the same manner as refusal to follow any reasonable request.

6. Staff should be authorized to assign juveniles evening chore assignments, i.e., rearranging furniture, emptying trash, cleaning. Evening chores should be rotated weekly among the juveniles.

7. Special cleaning activities should be periodically scheduled.

8. Unit and central service staff should make log entries, complete work orders, and take appropriate action when unhealthy or unsafe conditions exist.

The purpose of daily unit inspections is threefold:

• to ensure all unit and individual room/dorm chores have been completed thoroughly so that a high level of sanitary conditions is continuously maintained

• to ensure all juveniles learn to take pride in having good personal habits and maintaining their personal hygiene

• to ensure unhealthy or unsafe conditions are identified, corrected, and reported immediately

Keeping recreation areas, such as the gym floor, clean can prevent injuries.

Other Upkeep Programs Involving Juveniles

There are a few programs of upkeep outside the living units conducted by careworkers, maintenance personnel, and/or vocational instructors worth considering. All of these programs involve working with juveniles. Most of the programs do not pay the juveniles and are either work experience or designed vocational offerings. These programs include building and maintenance, painting, and floor covering (carpeting)—activities pertinent to the care of the physical plant. In some situations, the juvenile may be paid (as in stipend programs) for evening and weekend work with careworkers, cooks, and maintenance personnel.

Juveniles in corrections facilities seem to be more skill-deficient than ever before. Therefore, it is imperative for the careworker to conduct task breakdown and teach skills step-by-step. Teaching simple, routine behaviors, such as properly unplugging cords from electrical outlets, is extremely important. Too often, a juvenile will jerk or yank a cord from an outlet, rather than taking the time to walk over and remove the plug properly. This seemingly insignificant action often leads to damage that may cause a fire.

Common areas outside the housing unit usually include kitchen/dining, medical, vocational, recreation, and academic classroom areas. The needs of the food service and medical areas are best served through production schedules. Cleaning, sanitizing, and controlling the presence of vermin and pests are accomplished by establishing the details (who, what, where, and when) on a regular schedule for each task. Because of the functions performed, these areas need continuous maintenance.

The vocational and recreation areas are where many accidents occur in facilities. The implications

---

It is imperative for the careworker to conduct task breakdown and teach skills step-by-step.

---

of poor housekeeping in shop areas are obvious. What is often neglected is the recreation area, particularly the gym floor. Many juvenile injuries and workmen's compensation cases are directly

attributable to the "marble effect." This situation occurs in as little as one day when dust accumulates on the gym floor. Daily dust removal, at a minimum, is necessary.

Reviews and Inspections

A clean physical plant is essential to the overall safety, security, and predictability of the facility's environment. Staff must supervise all unit cleaning activities and, when appropriate, should teach basic skills in housekeeping and emphasize the importance of having sound personal hygiene habits.

Care of the physical plant by juveniles and staff is an important, comprehensive project requiring everyone's efforts to maintain excellent standards. To ensure the entire environment is properly maintained, the facility needs a regular compliance review. ACA Standard 3-JTS-4B-01 states: "Written policy, procedure, and practice require weekly sanitation inspections of all facility areas." The standard is critical not only to the care of physical plant, but it is also critical to staff and juveniles' attitudes and morale. A weekly health and safety committee review of all facility areas should be conducted, and a report should be submitted to the chief executive officer. At a minimum, the group should comprise someone in charge of operations, medical staff, a fire safety officer, and maintenance staff to record and process necessary repairs. It is beneficial to include unit administrators and area supervisors occasionally on a rotating basis to reinforce the significance of proper

Maintaining clean living areas is important to a juvenile's sense of pride and achievement.

care of their areas. Further, a written report of violations, necessary repairs, and areas needing improvement should be reviewed with all first-line supervisors. This process tends to produce a healthy competition and highlights the problems or issues that repeat.

One way to focus on cleanliness and hygiene is to conduct individual room inspections prior to breakfast every day. The issues of pride and practices in these areas are usually topics in meetings held on each unit before breakfast. Additionally, a weekly fire safety inspection should be conducted by trained staff. The process includes careworkers and is a mandatory ACA standard (3-JTS-3B-02).

Preventive Maintenance

According to ACA Standard 3-JTS-3B-08, there should be a "written plan for preventive maintenance of the physical plant; the plan includes provisions for emergency repairs or replacement in life-threatening situations....regular care and inspection of equipment is essential for safe and efficient operations." Generally, such items as power tools in shops or meat slicers in the kitchen come to mind when thinking of potentially dangerous equipment, but vacuum cleaners, buffers, and shampoo equipment can be just as dangerous if they are not properly maintained.

Another important preventative maintenance issue is the "vacant house, first broken window" effect. Once a window is broken in a vacant house, it seems to become an abandoned house, and juveniles are less inhibited in using other windows for "target practice." This phenomenon is just as applicable to graffiti, carving one's initials anywhere and everywhere, and leaving messes. Juvenile behavior reflects what is tolerated. If the marks of vandalism are removed immediately, the perpetrator is less likely to continue such behavior, and others are not likely to join in. Similarly, if juveniles are required to clean up messes immediately and reclean areas that were improperly cleaned in the first place, a high standard for the care of physical plant and self will evolve.

APPLICABLE ACA STANDARDS

3-JTS-2A-01–2604
3-JDF-2A-01–2602

13

Return to the Community

By David J. Riffe

Juveniles entering a detention facility or training school frequently ask two questions: "When do I get to go home?" and "What do I need to do to get out of here?" Careworkers and other staff play a major role in preparing juveniles for community placement. From intake through release,

---

Careworkers and other staff play a major role in preparing juveniles for community placement.

---

careworkers help juveniles by working on behavior, attitudes, fears, and anxieties about institutional living (the institutional program itself and other juveniles) and the prospect of going home. Careworkers must meet these needs by constantly motivating juveniles to perform properly in the institutional program.

The admissions process is when the encouragement for participation in the treatment program begins. Participation in treatment prepares

---

David J. Riffe is a consultant specializing in counseling services for juveniles and residential programs for dependent juveniles, juvenile corrections, and adult corrections.

juveniles for a return to the community. Individualized treatment plan goals require the careworker's input to the counselor and treatment team. Thorough individualized program plans use specific, measurable goals with time lines for completion. These indicate to juveniles what must be done to move toward more privileges and home placement. Encouragement, motivation, support, day-to-day direction, and informal counseling are major careworker roles to this end.

On completion of treatment plan goals or at the end of the juvenile's detention period, careworkers help the juvenile face leaving the known (institutional rules, staff, and other juveniles) and aid in the movement to the unknown—the community from which the juveniles came. These unknowns include family, friends, new authority figures, and a community that have changed during the juvenile's detention. In placement, juveniles experience a change of living environments, resources, and primary workers to which they must adjust.

Supervision by a parole officer or aftercare worker usually takes place on placement. Some systems use community residential programs for a halfway transition home—between institution and probation. Either of these options requires another adjustment to rules and authority figures.

Some systems use community residential programs for a halfway transition home.

The Roles of Institutional Staff

There are three major phases of staff aid to the juvenile returning to the community:

- intake process

- programming

- preparation for release

Within each of these phases, there are three major aspects on which most institutional staff focus:

- personal needs—the juvenile's feelings, emotions, motivation, fears, and anxieties

- preparation—the individualized program plan goals, achievement opportunities, counseling, skill learning, and guidance

- placement—planning, community and family linkages, communication, and placement coordination (the transition)

In a juvenile correctional institution, teachers must motivate the juvenile (perhaps for the first time in the juvenile's life) to strive for academic achievement. Recreation workers should help juveniles build self-confidence and self-esteem and teach them the value of teamwork. Work supervisors teach skills that build confidence and pride.

Counselors are responsible for overall case management, including programming, treatment team leadership, and individualized program plan goal development. Coordination of these goal plans with the juvenile helps focus on placement success. Counselors also provide counseling, direction, motivation, and outlets for feelings.

The careworker works with juveniles on the unit who share the same classification (similar age, size, offense, and problems). Careworkers are responsible for the daily living of juveniles on the unit and other activities on or off campus. This unit must be a positive, reinforcing group, giving "pats on the back," compliments, and encouragement. It must also give informal direction in following the treatment plan to a positive conclusion—community placement.

Intake

In some institutions the first staff a new admission comes in contact with is a careworker. This contact may be when the careworker transports the juvenile to the facility. Additionally, the careworker may provide the orientation review of rules. Introducing new admissions to other unit members and staff in the facility is a major role for the careworker during this stage. This intake orientation is essential for the juvenile who wants to participate properly and go home quickly.

Other staff may do the formal orientation, but the careworker's focus must be on "making it" in the facility and wanting to make it on the outside. The living unit is a primary place to encourage this.

Personal fears and anxieties about leaving home, meeting new people, and living under new rules and questions about what the juvenile needs to do to be allowed to go home and when he or she will be allowed to go home are frequently discussed in the living unit. There may be fear of isolation from home and community or anxiety about protection and safety in the facility. All staff must be aware of and deal with these issues to encourage positive behavior.

Careworker activities during orientation include reviewing the rules, contacting parents for visitation, and enforcing rules pertaining to phone calls and mail. Support and encouragement in each of these areas will lead to a positive programming stage. When juveniles face their programming in a positive manner, staff have significantly prepared them for release.

Discharge planning begins at the time of intake. Admissions personnel begin asking about family, siblings, communities, schools, and peer groups. The information gathered is noted on the juvenile's intake form, and copies of the form are made available to careworkers serving the juvenile's unit.

The interests, hobbies, sports, abilities, and fears of each juvenile become known to the careworker first. Well-run institutions get input from careworkers when developing the individualized program or treatment. Unit staff are often a major part of the treatment team for each juvenile's programming plan and review. They help give a complete picture of each juvenile.

Through informal discussions, letters, visits, phone calls, and unit problems, unit staff learn first-hand what placement problems will occur. They often hear about parental abuse, alcoholism, neglect, and other negatives about the home and community before counselors do. This information adds to the presentence reports submitted at intake by the sentencing authority.

To aid successful return to the community, staff must look at institutional adjustment skills and turn them into skills for living in the community. For example, unit staff should help differentiate between appropriate and inappropriate horseplay. This behavior is acceptable in the gym, but

---

Staff must look at institutional adjustment skills and turn them into skills for living in the community.

---

unacceptable in the dining room or during school. Another area is language. It is common for juveniles to use slang terms and to curse. Rather than completely prohibiting the use of this type of language, staff must help teach when, where, and with whom it is inappropriate. These examples show how important careworkers are in helping the juvenile achieve a smooth return to the community.

Focus on returning to the community must also be present in regard to behavior, attitudes,

The juvenile may want to discuss his anxieties about returning home.

language, and achievements. Staff "pats on the back" for achieving in school or compliments for work or shop projects go a long way in building esteem. Self-esteem is a major ingredient for a successful return to the community. Rewards should be given for completing individual program plan goals.

Prerelease Programs

Prerelease programs are different in each facility. Most of these programs are presented as separate classes or workshops and usually take an educational approach. They include social skills development, practical day-to-day economics, support and resource systems, and community services available. Topics are usually presented using one or more of the following techniques:

- lectures about the role of the aftercare/parole officer; laws of the community; and use of community services, such as Alcoholics Anonymous, Narcotics Anonymous, Al-ateen, Al-anon, child protective services, and neighborhood centers

- exercises in budgeting, completing job applications, interviewing for employment, using a checking and savings account, understanding taxes and filing tax forms, purchasing products and services, and developing independent living skills

- role playing and counseling in anger management, appropriate attitudes and language, dealing with authority, and acquiring tools for making it in the community

Prerelease efforts focus on the concerns of the soon-to-be-released juvenile. Counselors and aftercare officers begin relating specific behavior and attitude problems to community adjustment issues. Work begins or becomes more intense with parents (or other placement resources) in preparation for the return home. Trial visits in the transition phase allow the prerelease program counselor to identify problems or potential problems of placement. Group therapy frequently begins during this time and usually addresses placement fears and anxieties. Juveniles may have fears and anxieties about changes in themselves and in the community since they have been in the corrections facility.

Transition Phase

The transition phase is marked by a shift in individual programming. This is a critical phase and requires additional support because of the strong emotions surrounding this change. The transition is important because it means moving from the structured, abnormal environment of the institution to the unstructured, normal community environment—an environment in which the juvenile will have to make decisions.

To understand the importance of the transition, the careworker should visualize the life a juvenile leads in the institution. For three to six months the juvenile wakes up when told, stands for head counts, and follows a schedule as to when and how long to shower. Permission must be asked for restroom privileges, and all recreation, education, and leisure time is scheduled. The juvenile has little input as to the food served and must stand in line and take the food provided. The juvenile is

---

Self-esteem is a major ingredient for a successful return to the community.

---

scheduled to talk to counselors about problems. He or she may walk from one building to another only while in a supervised group. The juvenile must live in a unit with eight to twelve others. He or she has little opportunity to make his or her own decisions. When the juvenile is released into the community, this will all change.

Transition programming often begins at least six weeks before placement. Treatment goals and plans must be substantially met before entering this phase. As the juvenile enters the transition phase, programming emphasis should shift to allow for some independent decision making and more privileges. These privileges usually involve less direct supervision and more freedom of choice of activities in the facility. Contacts with the community and family also increase during this time.

Home visits usually begin or increase during this phase. The careworker may be assigned to contact the family to arrange the details of the visits. Parents usually ask about their child's attitude and behavior. Visits often run more smoothly when staff respond positively to parents' questions.

Juveniles' concerns, questions, and anxieties about what they will be faced with in terms of parents, community, and friends are often expressed on the unit—sometimes through acting-out behavior. As the day of the visit approaches, more questions and feelings may be expressed to staff, sometimes in unexpected times and places, such as at the pool table, in the hallway, or on the playing field; they may come

---

Juveniles may have fears and anxieties about changes in themselves and in the community since they have been in the corrections facility.

---

up in a classroom, at the careworker's desk, or at bedside. Providing reassurance, support, guidance, direction, and specific answers to questions is a major function of staff.

Juveniles often return from home visits feeling upset. On return to the institution, careworkers are frequently the only staff available to the juvenile. Unit staff should be alert to their actions and moods and should help them resolve their frustrations and anger.

Detailed, written notes about this interaction should be given to the treatment counselor. Anger may be based on feelings of rejection or pressure imposed by friends in the community or on changes in the home. There may be fears because of a parent's ongoing drinking problem. Conditions at home may cause the juvenile to wonder whether staff will approve home placement. The juvenile may have his or her own doubts about wanting to return to that environment. The careworker must communicate his or her interaction with the juveniles to treatment team members, who will help address any problems. The aftercare officer may investigate the juvenile's home and community. This officer will then have frequent contact with the family.

Some institutions schedule activities for juveniles that take place off the facility grounds during the later phases of the program. Juveniles may be allowed to participate in outside community recreational programs. Some facilities allow or encourage work, vocational, educational, and support services (i.e., Alcoholics Anonymous and Narcotics Anonymous meetings) in the nearby community.

Furloughs (extended home visits) are often available to help reorientation into the community. These programs help the juvenile "normalize" before placement. They help the soon-to-be-released juvenile learn to make his or her own decisions and to relate in a positive, community-oriented way to others. They also aid learning how to act appropriately in the community.

The transition program is based on the individualized program plan, and it takes into account behavior and attitude changes. Security risk and community safety must, however, come first. The aftercare officer often selects (or approves) the community employment or educational plans before placement. The officer also monitors use of resources, conduct, attendance, skills, attitudes, and achievements in these placements.

Placement may be suspended if a juvenile absconds or violates home visit rules. In such a case, another personalized goal and plan is developed to address problems apparent during placement.

Community Residential Halfway Houses

Some corrections systems use halfway houses to help juvenile offenders return gradually to the community. These are frequently less institution-like than standard corrections facilities. They are located in the community and can accommodate eight to twenty-five beds. Programming is not as restrictive as in the institution. Juveniles live in the facility, but have scheduled activities in the community. The length of stay in the halfway house may be from two to six months or more, depending on the juvenile's needs.

Staff in these community facilities have similar roles as staff in institutions. They help the juvenile adjust and prepare for more involvement in the community. Much of the juvenile's scheduling includes using community resources (schools, therapy, medical and dental services, recreation, vocational education, and employment). Services provided in the halfway house vary from many to very few. A primary counselor is assigned to each juvenile in the community residential program for case management.

Staff develop individualized program plan goals shortly after admission to the halfway house (usually within fourteen days). Goals stress the use of community resources, family contacts, and normalized community behavior.

A juvenile is placed in a halfway house that is located close to his or her own community to facilitate normalizing. Because they are living closer to home, home visits or family visits to the facility become more frequent. Phone contacts also increase during this phase of the program.

Family counseling (in-house or through a community resource) may begin on a regular basis. Transfer to a community residential program brings increased community, school, and family contact. During this phase, the juvenile receives progressively less direct supervision. Juveniles attend prerelease programs like those offered in the institution for further education and to help ease the transition to living in the community.

The Field Aftercare Officer

The role of the field aftercare officer is to guide and help the newly released juvenile adjust to living in the community.

The officer may be a state or county probation officer who also has parole responsibilities or a state or county parole officer having only aftercare responsibilities. Some systems use specially trained community workers called aftercare workers or community counselors.

Before release from the facility, the aftercare officer should visit the juvenile in the institution to begin the community return process. The reasons for this visit may include the following:

- begin or reestablish a relationship with the juvenile before release from the facility

- begin preparing an individualized program plan (release plan) for the juvenile

- orient the soon-to-be-released juvenile to the program and to the rules, rights, and regulations of aftercare

- gain information from facility staff to write a parole report for the parole board (if applicable)

Systems differ as to who provides transportation from the facility. Depending on the system, the

The careworker is sometimes responsible for escorting the juvenile home.

careworker, the family, or the aftercare officer transports the juvenile home.

The aftercare officer is sometimes responsible for working with the juvenile's family before the juvenile is returned home to help prepare the family. This contact may include monitoring trial home visits and working with the family on long- and short-term goals. The family is often given referrals to community service agencies for financial, housing, or employment help.

The facility counselor and aftercare officer coordinate placement plans and dates while helping to develop a release plan. The plan may include the following:

- attending Alcoholics Anonymous or Narcotics Anonymous meetings

- receiving individual and family counseling

- participating in vocational training

- participating in the education plan

- holding down a job

The plan may also consider the level of supervision the juvenile requires. The level system defines the number of contacts with the juvenile required by the aftercare officer per week. It forms the basis of the supervision plan for the juvenile while he or she is in the community.

Supervision by the aftercare officer will, ideally, consist of knowing the juvenile's whereabouts, activities, conduct, and attendance in required community activities. School and work contacts ensure program compliance. Proof of attendance at Alcoholics Anonymous or Narcotics Anonymous meetings or schools is also available. Regular family, school, employment, and peer contacts prove compliance of attendance. These contacts also determine alcohol or drug use and general attitudes and behavior.

The number of contacts with family, employer, or school depends on the supervision plan or need. Some level-of-supervision programs include specific time lines for each level; others base the levels on progress with goals. These levels of contact may range as follows:

- intensive—(first two weeks) four face-to-face contacts a week, with telephone contacts the other three days; one telephone contact with school or employer; and two telephone contacts with family

- medium—(weeks three through twelve) one face-to-face contact and one telephone contact per week, one telephone contact with school or employer per week, and one telephone contact with the family per week

- minimum—(week twelve through to release) one face-to-face contact per month, two telephone contacts with school or employer

per month, and two telephone contacts with the family per month

The aftercare officer writes a release summary showing successful completion of aftercare. The release may be an administrative process or may require a court appearance for judicial release. It may also require a recommendation for discharge to the paroling authority.

Unsuccessful completion of the juvenile's aftercare plan may lead to an administrative hearing or court review resulting in a new disposition. New charges, major violations, or absconding often requires a return to the institution.

Aftercare from institutions has traditionally been a weak area in juvenile services; if it was provided at all, it was by institutional staff or already overburdened court probation officers. It has been only within the past fifteen to twenty years that states have expressed an interest in aftercare. Parole and the use of aftercare officers is now a major emphasis in many states. Where parole systems are missing, states are increasingly providing aftercare supervision in the community by special probation officers. These officers may have regular probation cases, plus aftercare cases, but do not exceed the overall load of regular probation.

Summary

Careworkers, along with other staff, play a significant role in getting the juvenile ready for successful reentry to the community. This must begin at intake and continue to release. Positive attitudes, motivation, and help on focusing on leaving the institution are key roles of facility staff.

APPLICABLE ACA STANDARDS
3-JTS-5I-01–14
3-JDF-5H-01–07

14

Corrections' Untapped Resources: The Community's Volunteers

By J. Steven Smith, Ph.D.

This is the age of unpleasant fiscal realities. The corrections profession finds itself facing an ever-increasing demand for beds and offender services while public-sector budgets are shrinking. The corrections professional finds that he or she is being asked to do more with less. These are difficult times that require the professional to become creative and seek new resources that will allow him or her to continue proper services to juveniles and provide adequate protection of the public.

One resource often overlooked is the vast storehouse of community members interested in correctional clients. Clearly, the involvement of volunteers in all facets of human services is growing. During 1991, inquiries about volunteer services rose 28 percent in New York City and 20 percent in Houston (Colson 1992). Peter Drucker, writing for the *Wall Street Journal*, reports that in ten years two-thirds of American adults—120 million

persons—will want to work as nonprofit volunteers for five hours a week (Drucker 1991).

These individuals can provide high-quality services to correctional programs at a minimal cost. Many correctional programs actively seek volunteers to perform necessary staff functions, and programs have found that well-trained volunteers can provide a dependable source of high-quality manpower.

Initial Obstacles

There are problems with the use of volunteers, but most of these can be overcome with planning and supervision. Perhaps the most difficult problem is the initial reluctance of staff to begin a volunteer program. Those who are not in favor of a volunteer program tend to view volunteers as one of three types: the do-gooder, the bleeding heart, or the anarchist. Not one of these stereotypes is welcomed by corrections staff.

Do-gooders come to the agency motivated primarily by their needs to feel good about

J. Steven Smith, Ph.D., teaches criminal justice and criminology at Ball State University, Muncie, Indiana.

themselves. They want to feel warm and fuzzy about their time with juvenile offenders. They are naive about the realities of correctional work, and they are, for the most part, useless. Selection processes and a good interview will weed out do-gooders from the pool of volunteers.

Bleeding hearts, on the other hand, are often overly involved. They believe that if they love the juvenile enough, they will be able to "love them back to righteousness." They will want to take juveniles home with them at night, may give juveniles money, and will be constantly asking staff why they are so hard on these poor, misbegotten juveniles. The agency must provide strict supervision of volunteers to avoid the bleeding heart's misapplied care and concern.

Anarchists are interested in tearing the system down. They view the criminal justice system as oppressive and volunteer so they can gather information to prove what they believe to be the fascist nature of the justice system. Again, the interview and supervision process will help to weed out these people.

Like selecting paid staff, there is no substitute for a strong selection and supervision process to ensure that everyone working in a corrections program is competent and responsible. Effective corrections programs select staff, whether paid or volunteer, with great care.

Today's Volunteers

Based on the findings of several national research projects, it is clear that volunteers have become a major part of the corrections business. These researchers found that volunteers are for the most part educated or currently in school, young (in their thirties), and stable (most had been in their current

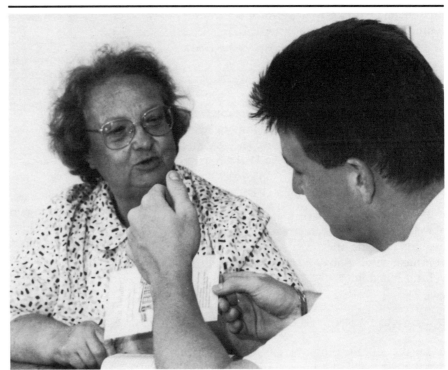

Volunteers are currently providing high-quality services across the nation.

volunteer capacity for two years or more) (Kratcoski et al. 1981). Today's volunteers are involved in a variety of correctional services, including probation and parole field supervision, educational services, court processing activities, case management, supervision of community service orders, victim-offender mediation, employment assistance, recreation services, counseling, alcohol treatment, stress management, anger control, substance abuse services, and advocacy services. Volunteers are currently providing professional-quality services across the nation (Nikkel 1988).

Developing a Volunteer Services Program

Careworkers should work with volunteers in the same way they work with paid employees. Maintaining this standard working relationship is critical to the success of the service program. Careworkers should not treat volunteers as second-class employees. Volunteers should be respected for their knowledge and skills. To develop this regular relationship, the agency must ensure that volunteers are prepared for the agency's mission and competent to perform the work required. Several important steps are required to accomplish this (McCarthy & McCarthy 1991).

Initial Planning

Agency administrators should involve careworkers, administrators, clients, and community members in the design of a volunteer program. This planning activity should ask questions like, Will it be effective? and How will it affect agency employees? Volunteers should not be used to replace necessary staff.

Planning should clearly state specific program objectives and should ensure each volunteer position has a detailed job description. A director of volunteer services may be necessary to coordinate volunteer activities.

Recruiting

At the onset of the program, the agency may find that it is difficult to locate volunteers. The agency must actively promote the program to attract them. Radio, television, newspapers, and civic groups are important recruitment options.

Screening

The screening process for volunteers should be similar to that for paid staff. Potential volunteers should be asked the following questions:

1. How much time can you devote to the program?

2. How well do you know the community? How well do you understand the criminal justice system?

3. What skills do you have? How would these skills meet the needs of the program?

4. Why are you applying for this volunteer position? What are your hobbies, civic involvement, and other outside interests? (The applicant's reason for applying is important, but it is also important for the volunteer to be a well-rounded role model for juveniles.)

5. What have you done in the past to develop attitudes, skills, and abilities useful for the correctional program? (Often sales experience or personal situations are important character builders for volunteers because the volunteer

can draw on these past experiences.)

6. How do you view the current state of society regarding juvenile crime and juvenile delinquents? (Volunteers need to understand the diversity of juvenile criminal behavior and juvenile delinquents.)

Training

Each volunteer should receive training in the job he or she is asked to perform. No facility would place paid staff into a position of authority over juveniles without training, and this same principle should apply to volunteers. Volunteers should receive training in the criminal justice system, understanding juvenile offenders, specific job responsibilities, community resources, and counseling.

Many volunteers will come to the job with mistaken beliefs about the facility or the program. The public is often misled by the media's portrayal

---

Volunteers should be respected for their knowledge and skills.

---

of sensational cases. Potential volunteers must be trained in the real operation and purpose of the criminal justice system.

Volunteers must understand the juveniles with whom they will be working. Staff should inform all volunteers about the types of juveniles housed in the facility or served by the program.

Volunteers must understand the specific role they are to play. They must be told the job duties as specifically as possible.

Volunteers should understand the other programs and services they can draw from to serve the juveniles. Information on the other services and programs of the sponsoring agency is important, but also important is knowledge about programs in the community that might be of assistance to either the juvenile or the volunteer.

Volunteers should not be asked to provide services that are too difficult for them. Training should ensure that the volunteer possesses the required level of skills for the position's requirements.

Volunteer/Offender/Supervisor Matching

A volunteer should be appropriately matched to the juvenile and to the supervisor. Information gathered during the selection, screening, and training phases should be appropriately assessed, and a suitable juvenile chosen for the volunteer. Likewise, a supervisor for the volunteer should be chosen who is compatible.

Working with a Volunteer

Staff who have a volunteer working with them should ensure that this person is nurtured and encouraged to develop his or her abilities. As the volunteer develops professional skills, the amount of work he or she can do increases. A volunteer can become an important member of the team in a correctional program.

The careworker can use a volunteer to work closely with a particular juvenile. This juvenile may be having particular difficulties adjusting to life in the institution, and the volunteer can spend extra time with him or her. Often the attention of a concerned volunteer is all that may be necessary to reduce a juvenile's anxiety and discomfort.

Volunteers are being used in a variety of settings, and they have shown a remarkable ability to develop into professional caregivers. Many programs and services are run entirely by volunteers, while other volunteers work alongside paid staff to supplement and support the system. A staff member's willingness to work with a volunteer will bring satisfaction to the staff member, the juvenile, and the volunteer.

Ending a Volunteer Relationship

Sometimes a volunteer must be asked to leave the agency. This should be handled carefully and with respect for the volunteer's dignity. Terminating a relationship with a volunteer should generally be handled like the termination of a paid employee.

When problems occur, the volunteer should be given the opportunity to correct his or her mistakes if possible. A well-trained volunteer will make fewer mistakes. When termination is necessary, the problems should be discussed with the volunteer, and staff should explain the reason for termination. Personnel files should be kept on volunteers, and commendations or suggestions should be formally noted.

Rewarding Volunteers

Although volunteers do not receive compensation for their services, they are "paid" in that they are doing something they enjoy. Most volunteers feel they are making an important, worthwhile contribution, and this feeling is a significant motivator. Staff must realize that to maximize the services of volunteers, they need to receive feedback about their work. Complimenting a volunteer for a particularly good decision or the successful

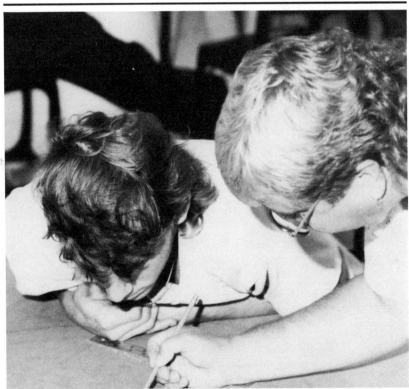

Matching the volunteer to the right juvenile is an important consideration.

completion of a difficult project is likely to be appreciated. Volunteers need to feel they are being successful in their efforts.

Summary

Shrinking budgets of correctional programs have reduced the ability of juvenile facilities to respond to the growing needs of detained and institutionalized juveniles. A growing portion of agency programs and services is being delivered by volunteers. With this growing need for volunteer services there seems to be a corresponding interest in volunteerism.

The selection and supervision of volunteers is similar to the proper development of paid staff. Both require a strong selection, training, and supervision process.

Staff who work with volunteers should be collegial and supportive. Volunteers should be treated like paid employees. They should have a detailed job description with specific duties and requirements. They should be encouraged to participate in agency-sponsored or -sanctioned training opportunities. It is important to match the volunteer with the juvenile, the supervisor, and the job duties.

A well-designed volunteer program will greatly enhance the agency's ability to address the needs of juveniles held in correctional institutions.

How to Get More Information

The National Association of Volunteers in Criminal Justice has developed several books and pamphlets on the effective use of volunteers. They can be contacted at NAVCJ, P.O. Box 786, Milwaukee, WI 35201.

Another growing organization of volunteers is Justice Fellowship (P.O. Box 17500, Washington, DC 20041-0500). They publish the *Justice Report*.

APPLICABLE ACA STANDARDS
3-JTS-1G-01–09
3-JDF-1G-O1–09

Bibliography

Abadinsky, H. 1979. *Social services in criminal justice*. Englewood Cliffs, N.J: Prentice-Hall.

Alexander-Rodriguez, T., and S. H. Vermund. 1987. Gonorrhea and syphilis in incarcerated urban adolescents: Prevalence and physical signs. *Pediatrics* 80: 561–64.

American Correctional Association. 1988. *AIDS in juvenile justice: A training program for juvenile careworkers*. Laurel, Md.: ACA. Videotape.

———. 1989. *Correctional officer resource guide*. Laurel, Md.: ACA.

———. 1988. *The critical hour: Admission in juvenile justice detention*. Laurel, Md.: ACA. Videotape.

———. 1992. *Guidelines for the development of policies and procedures: Juvenile detention facilities*. Laurel, Md.: ACA.

———. 1992. *Guidelines for the development of policies and procedures: Juvenile training schools*. Laurel, Md.: ACA.

———. 1992. *Handbook for juvenile justice advisory boards*. Laurel, Md.: ACA.

———. 1992. *Handbook on facility planning and design for juvenile corrections*. Laurel, Md.: ACA.

———. 1985. *Issues in juvenile delinquency*. Laurel, Md.: ACA.

———. 1986. *Juvenile careworker correspondence course*. Laurel, Md.: ACA.

———. 1992. *Juvenile justice in the United States: A video history*. Laurel, Md.: ACA. Videotape.

———. 1992. *National juvenile detention directory*. Laurel, Md.: ACA.

———. 1983. *Standards for juvenile community residential facilities*. 2d edition. Laurel, Md.: ACA.

———. 1991. *Standards for juvenile detention facilities*. 3d edition. Laurel, Md.: ACA.

———. 1983. *Standards for juvenile probation and aftercare services*. Laurel, Md.: ACA.

———. 1991. *Standards for juvenile training schools*. 3d edition. Laurel, Md.: ACA.

———. 1991. *Standards for small juvenile detention facilities*. Laurel, Md.: ACA.

———. 1990. *Suicide in juvenile justice facilities: The preventable tragedy*. Laurel, Md.: ACA. Videotape.

Armstrong, T. L., ed. 1991. *Intensive intervention with high-risk youths: Promising approaches in juvenile probation and parole*. Monsey, N.Y.: Criminal Justice Press.

Bayh, B. 1975. *Our nation's schools—A report card: "A" in school violence and vandalism*. Washington, D.C.: U.S. Senate.

Becker, H. S. 1963. *Outsiders: Studies in the sociology of deviance.* Glencoe, Ill.: Free Press.

Bernard, T. J. 1992. *The cycle of juvenile justice.* New York: Oxford University Press.

Binder, A., G. Geis, and D. Bruce. 1988. *Juvenile delinquency: Historical, cultural, legal perspectives.* New York: MacMillan.

Bolman, W. M. 1969. Toward realizing the prevention of mental illness. In *Progress in community mental health*, ed. L. Bellak & H. H. Barten. New York: Grune & Stratton.

Brady, M., C. Baker, and L. S. Neistein. 1988. Asymptomatic chlamydia trachomatous infections in teenage males. *Journal of Adolescent Health Care* 9: 72–75.

Caplan, G. 1964. *Principles of preventive psychiatry.* New York: Basic Books.

Cloward, R. A., and L. E. Ohlin. 1960. *Delinquents and opportunity.* New York: The Free Press.

Colson, C. W. 1992. A prophetic look at the profits of nonprofits. *The Justice Report* (Winter): 3.

Council on Scientific Affairs. 1990. Health status of detained and incarcerated youth. *Journal of the American Medical Association* 263: 987–91.

Cox, S. M., and J. J. Conrad. 1978. *Juvenile justice: A guide to practice and theory.* Dubuque, Iowa: William C. Brown Publishers.

Drucker, P. F. 1991. It profits us to strengthen nonprofits. *Wall Street Journal*, Dec. 19, p. 14A.

Eastern Kentucky University. 1990. *Transitional services for trouble youth.* Richmond, Ky.: Eastern Kentucky University.

Farrow, J. Medical responsibility to incarcerated children. *Clinical Pediatrics* 23: 694–700.

Federal Bureau of Investigation. 1975. *Uniform Crime Report.* Washington, D.C.: U.S. Government Printing Office.

Goldstein, A. P. 1990. *Delinquents on delinquency.* Champaign, Ill.: Research Press.

Goldstein, A. P., et al. 1989. *Reducing delinquency: Intervention in the community.* New York: Pergamon.

Goldstein A. P., and B. Glick. 1987. *Aggression replacement training.* Champaign, Ill.: Research Press.

Hein, K., et al. Juvenile detention: Another boundary issue for physicians. *Pediatrics* 66: 239–45.

Hirschi, T. 1969. *Causes of delinquency.* Berkeley, Calif.: University of California Press.

Hurst, H. 1990. Turn of the century: Rediscovering the value of juvenile treatment. *Corrections Today* 52 (February): 48–50.

Kratcoski, P., et al. 1981. Contemporary perspectives on correctional volunteerism. In *Correctional counseling and treatment*, ed. P. Kratcoski. Pacific Grove, Calif.: Brooks/Cole Publishing Company.

Lane, B. The relationship of learning disabilities to juvenile delinquency: Current status. *Journal of Learning Disabilities* 13: 20–29.

Lemert. 1967. *Human deviance, social problems, and social control.* Englewood Cliffs, N.J: Prentice-Hall.

Mahoney, A. R. 1987. *Juvenile justice in context.* Boston, Mass.: Northeastern University Press.

Mann, R. E., et al. 1985. A comparison of young drinking offenders with other adolescents. *Drug and Alcohol Dependence* 15: 181–91.

Marcus, R., and CDC Cooperative Needlestick Group. 1988. Surveillance of healthcare workers exposed to blood from patients infected with the human immunodeficiency virus. *New England Journal of Medicine* 319: 1118–23.

McCarthy, B. R., and B. J. McCarthy. 1991. *Community-based corrections.* 2d edition. Pacific Grove, Calif.: Brooks/Cole, pp. 370–99.

Meier, R. 1976. The new criminology: Continuity in criminological theory. *Journal of Criminal Law and Criminology* 67: 461–69.

Mikkel, R. W. 1988. *Guidelines for the effective design and management of volunteer involvement in juvenile and criminal justice.* Milwaukee, Wis.: National Association of Volunteers in Criminal Justice.

Miller, W. B. 1957. The impact of a community group work program on delinquent corner groups. *Social Services Review* 31, No. 4: 390–406.

Morgan, M. C., D. L. Wingand, and M. E. Felice. 1984. Subcultural differences in alcohol use among youth. *Journal of Adolescent Health Care* 5: 191–95.

National Association Against Media Violence. 1989. *Television violence and assault on our children.* Washington, D.C.: National Association Against Media Violence.

National Institute of Drug Abuse. 1990. *High school senior drug use: 1975–1989.* NIDA Capsules 1–4. Rockville, Md.: National Institute of Drug Abuse.

Nettler, G. 1974. *Explaining crime.* New York: McGraw-Hill.

Quinncy, R. 1974. *Critique of legal order: Crime control in capitalistic society.* Boston, Mass.: Little Brown.

Pizzo, P., and K. Butler. 1991. In the vertical transmission of HIV, timing may be everything. *New England Journal of Medicine* 325: 652–53.

President's Commission on Law Enforcement and Administration of Justice. 1967. *The challenge of crime in a free society.* Washington, D.C.: U.S. Government Printing Office.

Schur E. 1971. *Labeling deviant behavior: Its sociological implications.* New York: Random House.

Simonsen, C. 1991. *Juvenile justice in America.* 3d edition. New York: MacMillan.

Sutherland, E. H., and D. R. Cressey. 1970. *Principles of Criminology.* 8th edition. New York: J. B. Lippincott.

Toch, H., and K. Adams. 1989. *The disturbed violent offender.* New Haven, Conn.: Yale University Press.

Van de Perre, P., et al. 1991. Postnatal transmission of human immunodeficiency virus type 1 from mother to infant: A prospective cohort study in Kigali, Rwanda. *New England Journal of Medicine* 325: 593–98.

Werlin, E. L., and E. O'Brien. Attitude change and a prison health care experience. *Journal of Nursing Education* 23: 393–97.

Wolfgang, M. E., and F. Ferrecerti. 1967. *The subculture of violence.* London: Tavistock Publications.

Index

National Association of Volunteers in Criminal Justice, 112
National school breakfast program, 89
National school lunch program, 89
Nettler, G., 33
Neurotics, 70
Nonprivileged mail, 22
Nonverbal behavior, 44
Nurse, 76, 77, 78, 78
Nutrition, 88–89

O

Ohlin, L. E., 34
On-the-job training for the careworker, 18
Orientation, 51, 101–102
    handbook, 51
Overdose, drug, 67, 68, 76, 77

P

Paranoid personalities, 71
Parens patriae, 2, 3, 8, 20
Parenting skills, 57
Parole, 106
    officer, 100
Passive-aggressive personality, 70, 71
Passive-dependent personality, 70–71
Peers, 55, 102
Personal hygiene, 15
Personal property, inventory of, 49
Personal space, 44
Personality disorders, 70
Personality trait disturbances, 70–71
Pest control, 91, 98
Petition, 48
    parameters for recommending a, 10
Phobics, 70
Photographing juveniles, 50
Physical abuse, 49, 65, 69
Physical exam, 76, 86
Physical plant, maintenance of, 15, 25, 96–99
Placement problems in prerelease programs, 102, 103
Placing out, 3–4
Police, 8, 9, 49

records, 52
Postsecondary education, 56, 57
Poverty, 32, 69
Power struggle, 42
Praise
    giving, 40, 41–43
    structured, 40–41
Prerelease programs, 103, 105
    transition phase in, 103–104
Present era, 5–6
Privacy, right to, 11, 21, 22, 25, 77
Privileged mail, 22
Probation, 9, 12, 100
    officer, 48, 105, 106
Problem solving, 39, 44, 45
Program coordinator, careworker as, 14, 15
Program plan goals, individualized, 101, 102, 103, 104, 105 (see also *treatment plan goals*)
Programming, 13, 14, 23–25, 36, 51, 52, 54–62, 101, 102
Prompting, 43
Property damage, 41, 42
Prosecutor, 10, 12
Protection, 50, 51
Proximity, 43
Psychiatric
    evaluation, 70, 83
    patients, 78
Psychological testing, 51, 52
Psychotics, 70, 72
Punishment, 2, 5, 11, 25, 26, 38, 39, 45–47, 50

Q

Quinney, R., 35

R

Racism, 31–32
    institutional, 32
    personal, 31
Radical theory, 35
Recipes, 91
Recording information, 48–49, 50, 76
Recovery discussion, 45
Recreation, 11, 16, 24, 51, 60–61, 98, 101

Tuberculosis, 77, 84
Tutoring, 56, 57

U

U.S. Department of Agriculture, 89
U.S. Supreme Court, 5, 21, 22, 23, 26

V

Vandalism, 99
Violent subculture, 33
Visitation, 11, 21–22, 50, 102, 105
Visits, home, 104, 105
Vocational
    education, 56, 104 (see also *vocational training*)
    testing, 52, 57
    training, 12, 57, 97, 106 (see also *vocational education*)
Voice
    tone, 44

volume, 44
Volunteer program, 108, 109–111, 112
    initial planning for a, 110
Volunteers, 11, 51, 60, 62, 108–112
    recruiting, 110
    rewarding, 111–112
    screening, 110
    staff working with, 111
    supervision of, 109, 112
    terminating, 111
    training, 110

W

Wards of the court, 65
Weapons, 43, 49
Withdrawal from drugs, 66, 67, 68
Wolfgang, M. E., 33–34
Work, 25, 51, 57, 58, 59, 97, 101, 104, 106